OLDHAM ATHLETIC
On This Day

OLDHAM ATHLETIC
On This Day

History, Facts & Figures
from Every Day of the Year

DAVE MOORE

OLDHAM ATHLETIC
On This Day

History, Facts & Figures from Every Day of the Year

All statistics, facts and figures are correct as of 31st August 2008

© Dave Moore

Published By:
Pitch Publishing Ltd,
A2 Yeoman Gate,
Durrington BN13 3QZ

Email: info@pitchpublishing.co.uk
Web: www.pitchpublishing.co.uk

First published 2008

A catalogue record for this book is available from the British Library.

10-digit ISBN: 1-9054112-9-4
13-digit ISBN: 978-1-9054112-9-0
Printed and bound in Great Britain by Cromwell Press

This book is dedicated to the memory of the great 1960s team of the Bobby Johnstone era, which brought me so much pleasure as a young fan.

Dave Moore – September 2008

FOREWORD BY CARL VALENTINE

Oldham Athletic is a family-orientated club steeped in history which dates back to their formation as Pine Villa in 1895. The club has seen many highs and lows along their journey and have been runners up at the highest level, as well as having to apply for re-election to the league. In between have been memories which have stimulated every emotion possible for the directors, players and the spectators of this homely Lancashire club.

Championships, promotions, big cup games, relegation, record wins and defeats, giant killings, players coming and going, capacity gates, all-time lows and a first trip to Wembley are just some of the fascinating facts that are contained in Dave's first book on Oldham Athletic Football Club.

It is nearly every young boy's dream in England to play professional football, and mine was realised when I signed for Oldham. But only a slice of fortune made it happen. As a 16-year-old I had a trial at Stockport County – it did not go well. My good friend Steve Massey was accepted, and I was not. Not knowing what to do, I proceeded to continue my education and take my A-levels, with the hope of becoming a PE teacher.

After a surprisingly good first year, my good friend Gary Riley asked if I would like to come to Oldham (to keep him company on the three buses he used to take) and see if he could get me a trial. I said "yes" and was introduced to coach Billy Urmston. I did not think I had made a good impression as I was invited to play in the 'B' team on the left wing. For those that remember me, my left leg was for standing on. That summer I played some of my best football ever, and even scored with my left foot. That was when the scout Colin MacDonald asked to speak to me and my parents. I was offered my first contract of £16 a week, of which half went to my Mum and Dad.

Some of my fondest memories are when I played for the youth team. We went on a run beating Manchester City (away), Everton (away), and Liverpool (home). It was stopped by Crystal Palace (away). That was mainly because the scout had told Billy Urmston that they were not very good. Little did we know we were playing Terry Venables' supposed team of the Eighties, with Kenny Samson and Vince Hilaire starring for them!

It is most appropriate that Dave has undertaken this venture as the team enter a new era. The old Oldham Athletic were within hours of not existing and the new Oldham Athletic (2004) finally seem to be heading in the right direction, starting to put the smiles back on the faces of their long-suffering supporters.

The book contains facts, figures and trivia to cover some of the more eventful happenings over the last century. It is laid out in a simple format, day by day for every day of the year, which is easy to read and will become the perfect companion for all true Latics fans as it can be read every day throughout the coming years.

Carl Valentine, Oldham Athletic 1976–80

INTRODUCTION

Oldham Athletic On This Day is a chronological record of facts, figures and trivia that have occurred on every day of the year during the life of Oldham Athletic and their fledgling club, Pine Villa. Athletic is a homely Lancashire club, which has brought love, misery, delight, despair, disgust, anger, sympathy, surprise and a whole range of other emotions to all their true followers. All Oldham fans will have experienced them all in some capacity – it's what supporting Oldham is about!

Athletic have experienced football at the highest level but have also had to contend with the embarrassment of having to apply for re-election to the league on more than one occasion. It's been a rollercoaster of a ride throughout the history of the club since the inception of Pine Villa in 1897.

The book begins on 1st January and continues through to 31st December and is a fascinating collection of happenings; some good, some not so good. January tells of many cup games and some major giant killing events, big after-Christmas games and record league gates and runs. February mentions famous managers and the 'St. Valentine's Day massacre'. March and April recognises new managers, manager dismissals and further big cup games. The summer months celebrate championships, suffer relegations, and applaud new players arriving, as well as old players departing. August is the time when all teams think that this will be 'their year' and the new seasons' aspirations and perspirations are all examined. Births and deaths are recorded throughout the year as are exceptional scores, transfers, individual feats, quotations, unscrupulous owners, debuts and a plethora of other interesting facts. When December arrives we are back at big cup games and Boxing Day encounters with some remarkable records being set.

It has been a labour of love gathering all the facts together and many hours of 'midnight oil burning' have been experienced in compiling the results. I sincerely hope that you enjoy reading *Oldham Athletic: On This Day*, and if you get half the enjoyment reading it as I have had writing it, I will feel that it has all been worthwhile.

Dave Moore – September 2008

ACKNOWLEDGEMENTS

I would like to thank the following for their encouragement and help in writing *Oldham Athletic On This Day*. Sincere thanks go to all my friends who have endured my company over the years that I have supported Oldham and to those who have travelled with me to the many away games since the 1959/60 season. There are too many people to mention individually but the ones who have been around the longest are Phil Stevenson, Barry Noble and Richard Gaskell. Richard became my adopted nephew who used to attend Boundary Park as a young nipper with his Uncle Phil and still does to this day. Those three deserve a special mention as they have continued to provide newspaper cuttings, programmes and other sundry Athletic related ephemera long before the Internet became such a valuable source of information. Dan Tester, author of *Brighton & Hove Albion: On This Day*, was responsible for initially suggesting that I should write the book and I am grateful for his help and encouragement. Thanks also go to the websites of Oldham Athletic (official), Oldham Athletic Mad and the Latics Supporters Club, Canada which have all provided accurate information. I appreciate the help of Alan Hardy and Oldham Athletic Football Club for their permission to use the official Oldham Athletic logo. Ross Coyne deserves a special mention for his excellent match reports as does Tony Snowden who sent his personal records of events and data about the Rhodesia and Malawi tour. Garth Dykes' books, *Oldham Athletic: A Complete Record 1899-1988* and *The Legends of Oldham Athletic* have been invaluable, as have Stewart W Beckett's *The Team From A Town Of Chimneys* and *Keeping The Dream Alive*. I became acquainted with John Leigh when he was writing his book about my all-time favourite Latics player, the great Bobby Johnstone, and my small contribution to that book, *Bobby Johnstone: The Passing Of An Age*, may just have inspired my subconscious, so he deserves credit for that. Thanks also go to my fellow Canadian Carl Valentine who provided the foreword for my book. Still revered in Oldham, he opted to represent Canada and was lucky enough to represent them in the 1986 World Cup finals. Last but not least, thanks to my family. My grown-up children have, when little, occasionally had to take a back seat in my pursuit of following Athletic. My late father Jack and late father-in-law Harry also made many road trips with me, and my wife Sandra has been her usual supportive and patient self while I have been compiling the book. My sincerest gratitude to you all.

Dave Moore – September 2008

OLDHAM ATHLETIC
On This Day

JANUARY

SATURDAY 1st JANUARY 1898

A trip to Hollinwood Onwards was the journey for Pine Villa in this Oldham Junior Association League Second Division game and they came away with a 2-1 win. The scorers were not recorded.

TUESDAY 1st JANUARY 1991

New Year's Day brought Newcastle United to Oldham. It looked like the visitors were returning with all the points until a bizarre own goal by Mark Stimson, with just 13 seconds of play left, gave Athletic a share of the points.

WEDNESDAY 1st JANUARY 2003

The New Year fixture at Prenton Park brought 9,795 hardy fans to watch Athletic extend their unbeaten away record to 13 games. A David Eyres penalty and a Julian Baudet goal gave the visitors a 2-1 victory over Tranmere Rovers.

MONDAY 1st JANUARY 2007

Nottingham Forest were the visitors for this top-of-the-table clash. A stunning performance from the Latics saw them rack up their biggest win of the season as they hammered the City Ground outfit by 5-0. Goals from Paul Warne, Chris Porter, David Rocastle and a brace from Andy Liddell were enough to see Athletic leap-frog Forest into an automatic promotion place. The game was played in front of 9,768 supporters.

TUESDAY 1st JANUARY 2008

In front of 25,906 supporters at Elland Road, Athletic inflicted Leeds United's first home defeat of the season. Strikes from Reuben Hazell, Neal Trotman and an own goal gave the Latics a 3-1 win – their sixth successive away victory.

SUNDAY 2nd JANUARY 1977

Centre-forward Stewart Littlewood died in Rotherham. Signed from Port Vale in 1929 for £1,300, he scored many important goals for Athletic. He scored 48 goals in 81 starts, a great average, before going back to Port Vale for a record fee of £1,550. He also scored six goals for Vale against Chesterfield when they recorded their record win of 9-1 in 1932.

SATURDAY 2ND JANUARY 1988

Athletic completed their first double of the season with a thumping 5-0 win at Bramall Lane. Frankie Bunn scored two goals while Mike Flynn, Tommy Wright and Roger Palmer administered the killer punches. Embarrassed Sheffield United manager Billy McEwan resigned his position straight after the final whistle.

SUNDAY 3RD JANUARY 1960

Nick Sinclair was born in Manchester. He made 75 appearances which was restricted due to many injuries. He scored one goal. His most memorable and important games included playing at Newcastle United against Keegan and Waddle, and against Manchester City at Maine Road. He left Oldham in 1984 and joined Tranmere Rovers. He finished playing in 1986 due to a pelvic injury related to a knee ligament problem.

SATURDAY 4TH JANUARY 2003

Peterborough United brought their team to Boundary Park and walked away with a surprise point in a 0-0 draw. Athletic were boasting an unbeaten away record but were struggling at home and another poor performance in a dull game didn't deserve anything more than a point.

SATURDAY 5TH JANUARY 2008

A huge away following were at Goodison Park to see Athletic take on Premiership side Everton in the third round of the FA Cup. Bizarrely a blaze in a chip shop outside the ground delayed the kick-off by half an hour – but it was League One Athletic, on the back of six successive away wins, who were on fire when play finally started. As expected, Everton dominated the main share of possession but on the stroke of half-time Gary McDonald unleashed a rocket shot to stun the Toffees supporters and give the Latics the shock result of the round in front of a 33,086 crowd.

SUNDAY 6TH JANUARY 1974

The Latics played the first ever senior game on a Sunday when they travelled to Cambridge United for an FA Cup tie. The match kicked off in the morning and an Abbey Stadium crowd of 8,479 supporters witnessed the historical fixture. The final score was 2-2.

MONDAY 6th JANUARY 1986

Fourth Division Orient were the visitors to Boundary Park for a third round FA Cup game and embarrassed Athletic by winning 2-1. The club's all-time leading scorer Roger Palmer got the Latics' goal on the day, but it was far from enough to see them win through to the fourth round.

SATURDAY 6th JANUARY 1990

Oldham travelled to St Andrew's to take on Birmingham in the third round of the FA Cup. With a home game beckoning in the fourth round for the winners of this tie, Joe Royle's men battled bravely and came away with a creditable 1-1 draw and another chance to see off Birmingham in the home return. Frankie Bunn got the important equalising goal.

SATURDAY 6th JANUARY 2007

A crowd of 14,524 were at Molineux for Athletic's third round FA Cup tie against Championship outfit Wolverhampton Wanderers. Paul Warne put the Latics ahead in the 19th minute but the Wolves fought back to take a 2-1 lead. Chris Hall popped up with a 78th minute header to earn the Latics a replay at Boundary Park, but Wolves won the tie 2-0.

SATURDAY 7th JANUARY 1905

Newton-le-Willows visited Hudson Fold in a Lancashire Combination 'B' Division game and returned home stinging from an 11-0 hammering. In one of the strangest ever goalscoring feats, centre-forward Plumpton scored the first five goals. Even stranger, the next six goals were all scored by inside-right Shoreman. '2,000' spectators watched the game.

SATURDAY 7th JANUARY 1950

Newcastle United, led by their legendary forward Jackie Milburn, visited Boundary Park for a third-round FA Cup game. The Magpies ran riot and beat the Latics by seven goals to two to end Athletic's Wembley dreams for another season.

SATURDAY 7TH JANUARY 1995

The Latics went to Reading for a third-round FA Cup tie and came away with a convincing 3-1 win. Reading had beaten the Athletic at Boundary Park earlier in the season when Joe Royle was in charge but this win came under new boss Graeme Sharp. The visitors' goals were hit by Sharp, Lee Richardson and Gunnar Halle.

WEDNESDAY 8TH JANUARY 1941

Goalkeeper Ron Swan was born in Plean, Stirlingshire. He made 64 appearances in his two years at the club in the sixties and shared the keeper's job with Johnny Bollands before being ousted by David Best. He began his career as an outfield player but was in goal for East Stirling when they won promotion to the First Division.

THURSDAY 8TH JANUARY 1942

Latics captain Bill Cranston was born in Kilmarnock. With 100 first team league games and two goals, Cranston became a Boundary Park favourite with his robust and physical defending. He was a member of Jimmy Frizzell's Fourth Division promotion-winning side and it's no coincidence that the fortunes of Athletic improved when he signed from Preston North End for a fee of £6,000 in 1970.

SATURDAY 8TH JANUARY 1949

Athletic bowed out of the third round of the FA Cup to Cardiff City by a 3-2 scoreline. An unbelievable gate of 28,991 watched the game. Few Third Division (North) clubs could compete with the number of spectators that Athletic were pulling in. An average of 14,500 watched the Latics that season.

SATURDAY 8TH JANUARY 2005

A memorable day for the Latics as Premiership side Manchester City visited Boundary Park in the third round of the FA Cup. They were put to the sword as Scott Vernon scored the only goal of the game, which was watched by a bumper gate in excess of 13,000. It was a day to forget for Kevin Keegan however, as the result was the final nail in the City manager's coffin, as the former England boss was sacked shortly after what the City board considered an extremely disappointing result.

WEDNESDAY 9TH JANUARY 1985

Liverpool paid Oldham a record fee received of £250,000 to take 17-year-old Wayne Harrison to Anfield. Manager Joe Royle arranged to take Harrison back on loan for the rest of the season in a deal which was unique at the time.

SATURDAY 9TH JANUARY 1988

First Division Tottenham Hotspur were in town for a third-round FA Cup game which attracted 16,931 visitors to Boundary Park. Tommy Wright and Mike Cecere scored the Athletic goals but they still bowed out by a 2-4 scoreline to their superior counterparts.

MONDAY 10TH JANUARY 1966

Tommy Wright was born in Dunfermline. Signed from Leeds United for £80,000 in 1986 he soon established himself as a great winger who was responsible for setting up many goals. He had been a member of the Scotland under-21 squad at the age of 18 and he is currently assistant manager to John Sheridan.

MONDAY 10TH JANUARY 1976

In their first season back in the Second Division after a gap of 20 years, the Latics struggled to maintain any consistency but a 3-0 win at Chelsea was a great boost to their confidence. David Shaw scored a memorable volley for the second goal of the game.

WEDNESDAY 10TH JANUARY 1990

This tense third round FA Cup replay at home to Birmingham City looked to be heading for a period of extra time, with neither team able to break the deadlock. However Rick Holden had other ideas, as he gathered the ball just outside the box, ran through three challenges and poked the ball home to earn Athletic a home game against Brighton, their first venture to the fourth round in five years.

SATURDAY 11TH JANUARY 1913

Bolton Wanderers visited a bitterly cold and snow-covered Boundary Park for a third round FA Cup game. Oliver Tummon scored twice to give the Latics a 2-0 win and set up a fourth round tie at home to Nottingham Forest.

SATURDAY 12TH JANUARY 1924

First Division Sunderland, the then favourites for the Football League Championship, visited Second Division Athletic for a first round FA Cup match. A bumper crowd of 24,726 showed up to watch the game and the home fans got the perfect start when Johnny Blair put the Athletic ahead in the ninth minute. Chris Staniforth added a second goal in the 38th minute to stun Sunderland's star studded team. Charlie Buchan – who at the end of his career found further fame as a journalist – pulled one back for Sunderland with 15 minutes to go but the Latics held on for a famous victory. The Mackems finished third in the First Division that season.

SATURDAY 12TH JANUARY 1974

Athletic began a memorable run of consecutive victories with a 2-1 win at Wrexham, on a day when goalkeeper Chris Ogden had one of his best-ever games to keep the Welsh club's forwards at bay. The club went on to win a record ten consecutive league games, a run ended by a 1-0 defeat at Chesterfield. The run helped Athletic claw back the incredible 13-point gap between them and Third Division leaders Bristol Rovers, as Oldham ended the season as champions.

SATURDAY 12TH JANUARY 1991

An amazing 4-1 win at Fratton Park completed another double as an incredibly good season continued for Athletic. Ian Marshall returned after injury to score twice, while Rick Holden and Roger Palmer completed the scoring to leave Athletic in the very healthy position of second spot in the Second Division.

WEDNESDAY 13TH JANUARY 1932

After a 1-1 draw at Boundary Park, Oldham faced a third round FA Cup replay at Leeds Road. It was a day to forget as Athletic were on the wrong end of a 6-0 thrashing by Huddersfield Town in a game witnessed by 20,609 fans.

SATURDAY 13TH JANUARY 1951

A crowd of 14,397 turned up to watch Athletic take on Carlisle United. Albert Wadsworth scored the Latics goal in a 1-1 draw which still left the blues joint bottom of the Third Division (North).

MONDAY 14th JANUARY 1884

Evergreen David Wilson was born in Irvine, Ayrshire. He was one of the best half-backs to play for Athletic. He played for the club from 1906 until 1921 and appeared in 405 games, scoring 20 goals. Wilson set a Football League record of 263 consecutive appearances – an amazing achievement, and he was still playing for Nelson in the Second Division at the age of 40.

MONDAY 14th JANUARY 1974

Athletic visited the City Ground in Nottingham to take on Cambridge United in a third-round FA Cup second replay. A goal by Andy Lochhead, and an own goal by Simmons, resulted in a 2-2 draw at Cambridge in the first game. The replay at Oldham was a great tie which was 2-2 at full-time, and 3-3 after extra time. George McVitie scored and Ian Robins got two to contribute to a marathon third game on the neutral ground. George Jones and Colin Garwood scored at Nottingham to ensure a 2-1 win and passage through to the fourth round.

SATURDAY 14th JANUARY 1989

Neil Adams – on loan from Everton – made his debut for Athletic in the home game against Manchester City. The Sky Blues won the game 1-0 and left the Latics struggling in 21st place in the Second Division. Adams played nine games during his loan spell, helping Oldham away from trouble, and eventually signed for Athletic that summer for a £100,000 fee. He played over 200 games for the club over two separate spells, from 1989 to 1994 and 1999 to 2001.

TUESDAY 14th JANUARY 2003

Three points were the order of the day after a 2-1 win over Brentford although they came in remarkable circumstances in a match marred by some incredulous refereeing decisions from official Mark Clattenburg. Fitz Hall headed the Latics in front from a John Sheridan corner in the 18th minute only for the Bees to equalise by a bizarre goal which came off a defender. Lee Duxbury regained the lead with a diving header. Clattenburg handed out six yellow cards in a silly 15-minute spell and to make matter worse, dismissed Latics keeper Les Pogliacomi with 30 seconds left on the clock!

THURSDAY 15TH JANUARY 1948

Record-breaking Ian Wood was born in Radcliffe. Signed as an amateur centre-forward by Gordon Hurst, Wood was a product of Athletic's youth system. Under Jimmy McIlroy's guidance he was converted from wing-half to full-back and this was the turning point in his career as he went from strength to strength. He was a dedicated professional and is the current holder of the club's all-time appearance record with an amazing 570 run-outs to his name. He was a member of the Third Division championship-winning team. He scored 26 goals in his time at Oldham and also had an unbroken run of 161 games to his credit.

SUNDAY 16TH JANUARY 1881

Full-back Billy Cook was born in Preston and scored 16 goals in 171 appearances for the Latics. He was sent off in a match at Glossop in 1910 for a foul and, as a result, was suspended for two months. In 1915 he was sent off again at Middlesbrough for a foul on Jack Carr. He refused to leave the field as he was convinced that he was innocent and the referee abandoned the game after 59 minutes with Athletic trailing 4-1. The FA subsequently ruled that the result should stand and Cook was given a 12-month ban. He played his last game for Athletic on 26th April 1920 and joined Rossendale United on a free transfer in August. Billy died in 1949 at Burnley.

SATURDAY 17TH JANUARY 2004

A gate of over 9,000 watched Athletic entertain Sheffield Wednesday in this League One game. Scott Vernon got the only goal with a header from an Adam Griffith centre to give the Latics a crucial 1-0 home win. Former Owls ace John Sheridan received a standing ovation from both sets of fans when he walked off the field in the 90th minute.

SATURDAY 18TH JANUARY 2003

The season's unbeaten away record in League One was maintained with a 2-2 draw at Wycombe Wanderers. Wayne Andrews opened the scoring, Wanderers hit back to go 2-1 up in the 83rd minute, and Tony Carr equalised a minute later.. The result was a good one, especially considering the Latics played most of the second half with ten men, after referee Clive Penton dismissed Julian Baudet two minutes into the second half.

SATURDAY 19TH JANUARY 1952

Athletic entertained Chester at Boundary Park in Arctic-like conditions. Sixteen-year-old Eddie Hopkinson, who went on to play for England, made two early blunders to set Chester up with a 2-1 lead in the first half hour of the game. But it was 30-year-old Eric Gemmell who took the glory from the match. In an amazing turnaround, Gemmell hit seven goals – six in succession, still a record for any Oldham player – as the Latics went on to win the game 11-2 in front of 13,458 delirious supporters. Athletic topped the average gate attendances for the season, both home and away, for the Third Division (North). Over the season an incredible average of 16,033 supporters were recorded for the home games.

FRIDAY 19TH JANUARY 1973

A 2-2 draw at home to Shrewsbury Town was enough to ensure that Athletic topped the Third Division table. David Shaw had been signed by West Bromwich Albion for a fee of £80,000 and Latics fans wondered where the goals would be coming from but Athletic still managed to finish the season in fourth place. Ian Wood, Keith Hicks and Maurice Whittle were all ever-presents in the team for the season.

SATURDAY 19TH JANUARY 1991

The huge travelling support for the visit of promotion rivals Barnsley caused Athletic fans to be moved from the Rochdale Road end of the ground. It left 13,000 seats for home fans, which was considered adequate. Athletic won the game 2-0.

WEDNESDAY 20TH JANUARY 1909

After a 1-1 draw at Boundary Park, the Latics travelled to Leeds City for an FA Cup replay. A gate of 19,097 watched City defeat Athletic 2-0.

SATURDAY 20TH JANUARY 2007

Ex-Latics player Wayne Andrews was on target at Boundary Park on his debut for Bristol City. Athletic had not lost at home since August but were ripped apart and couldn't complain about the 3-0 defeat. The win took City into second place, two positions above the Latics.

MONDAY 21st JANUARY 1924

Goalscorer Don Travis was born in Moston. The converted centre-back stood 6ft 3in and weighed 13 stone. He gave defenders a tough time as he was very nimble for his size with a terrific left foot. He had two spells with Athletic and made 118 league appearances while netting 62 goals. In the 1954/55 season he scored 32 times, just one short of equalling Tommy Smith's record of 33 which was set in 1935-36. Don died in Yeovil in February 2002.

SATURDAY 22nd JANUARY 1966

West Ham United came to a packed Boundary Park for a third round FA Cup tie. It was a great game of football which ended 2-2. Reg Blore got the first goal to put Athletic ahead but the home side should have won the game as Albert Quixall had a penalty saved. Two days later the Latics went to Upton Park for the replay but lost 2-1 and ended their interest in the cup for another season.

TUESDAY 22nd JANUARY 2008

The 0-0 draw at Gillingham, watched by 4,402 supporters, was Athletic's ninth consecutive away game without defeat, a club record.

SATURDAY 23rd JANUARY 1993

A 3-0 defeat against Coventry City at Highfield Road left Athletic next to the bottom of the Premier League. It was the only Premiership fixture played that day, and disappointingly a win would have lifted Athletic out of the relegation positions.

TUESDAY 23rd JANUARY 1996

After a 1-1 draw at Oakwell, Athletic brought Barnsley back to Oldham for this FA Cup third round replay. The Latics dispatched their Yorkshire counterparts with a 2-1 win after a brace from Darren Beckford. Neil Redfearn notched the away side's reply.

TUESDAY 24th JANUARY 1961

Paul Heaton was born in Hyde. A tricky dribbler who scored 28 goals in 136 league games, he appeared in midfield, on the wing and at full-back for Athletic after he had made his debut at the tender age of 17. He left in 1984 to team up with Vic Halom at neighbours Rochdale.

TUESDAY 24TH JANUARY 1984

Stocky Stockport County striker Micky Quinn signed for Athletic in a £52,000 deal. The Liverpool-born centre-forward scored 34 goals in 80 appearances before being sold to Portsmouth for £150,000 in 1986.

WEDNESDAY 24TH JANUARY 1990

Athletic made their first-ever appearance in the League Cup quarter-finals at The Dell. Southampton took the lead through Saints star player Matt Le Tissier but a powerful header from Andy Ritchie drew Athletic level. With five minutes of time remaining Saints were awarded a penalty, which Le Tissier competently dispatched to put them 2-1 ahead. Understandably, Southampton tried to play out the game by running the clock down, but referee Roger Milford punished them by adding on four minutes of additional time. In the fourth minute of injury time – and with the Saints fans celebrating victory – Rick Holden centred for Ritchie to poke home a dramatic last gasp equaliser to send the tie to a replay. Several hundred of the thousands of Latics fans who made the trip to Southampton couldn't get in, as 21,026 fans filled the ground to capacity.

SATURDAY 25TH JANUARY 1930

The all-time record gate for a match at Boundary Park was established when 46,471 people crammed in to watch the FA Cup fourth round tie with Sheffield Wednesday, who won an entertaining game 4-3, the winning goal was scored by Jack Allen with the last kick of the game.

SATURDAY 25TH JANUARY 1964

Athletic – in the hunt for back-to-back promotions – lost 1-0 at Crewe Alexandra in the Third Division. Under new boss Les McDowall they had been in the top two all season, but this defeat started a disastrous run which saw the Latics on a downward spiral. The next 12 games yielded just six points and included seven home defeats. They finished the season 12 points behind the promoted pair of Coventry and Crystal Palace.

FRIDAY 26TH JANUARY 1940

Centre-forward Frank Large was born in Leeds. The big bustling striker hit 18 goals in 34 league starts but was then transferred to Northampton Town for £14,000, almost double what the Latics had paid Carlisle United for his services the year previously.

SATURDAY 26TH JANUARY 2008

Huddersfield Town, managed by Oldham legend Andy Ritchie, were at Boundary Park for a fourth round FA Cup tie. It was a battle of the giant-killers, as both sides had disposed of Premiership opposition in the third round – the Latics winning at Everton and the Terriers seeing off Birmingham City. A gate of 12,749 saw Oldham old boy Luke Beckett score the only goal of the game in the tenth minute, as Oldham missed out on a money-spinning fifth round trip to Premiership Chelsea.

SATURDAY 27TH JANUARY 1962

A huge game at Boundary Park as the mighty Liverpool came to town for a fourth round FA Cup tie. A massive 41,733 crowd crammed into the ground to see the Reds edge the game 2-1. Liverpool took the lead in controversial fashion in the 73rd minute when Ian St John scored an in-off-the-bar goal, reminiscent of Geoff Hurst's disputed 1966 World Cup Final goal. St John got a second in the 80th minute before John Colquhoun replied for the Latics in the 83rd minute to set up a nail-biting final few minutes for the visitors. That season Liverpool won the Second Division championship.

SATURDAY 27TH JANUARY 1990

Athletic were going well in the cups and the games were coming thick and fast. They faced a fifth-round replay in the League Cup, having drawn at Southampton a few days earlier, but on this day were in FA Cup action. Brighton & Hove Albion were the visitors for a fifth round tie, only Athletic's second time at this stage in 11 years. Ian Marshall was switched from defence to attack, by then a familiar tactic employed by Joe Royle, and one which had been paying dividends. The visitors took the lead through Mark Barham but Scott McGarvey hit a left footer in the 66th minute to level the scores. Just two minutes later the majority of the 11,034 crowd went wild as Andy Ritchie powered a header wide of future Latic John Keeley for a place in the last 16 of the cup.

SATURDAY 28TH JANUARY 1928

White Hart Lane was the venue for Athletic who took on Tottenham Hotspur in the FA Cup. Spurs won 3-0 in front of 36,826 supporters who paid decent receipts of £2,720. The Latics were depleted with injuries and finished the game with only eight men on the field.

THURSDAY 28TH JANUARY 1926

Bill Spurdle was born in St. Peter Port, Guernsey. He had two spells at the Latics and was signed second time around from Port Vale for a fee of £1,000 in 1957. He came to Oldham as an evacuee from Guernsey during the Second World War. He also appeared in the FA Cup Final for Manchester City in 1955. Most of his appearances were from the right-half position and he was remembered for his long stride which gave him his speed. He notched 28 goals in 218 games and returned to Guernsey on retirement from the game to start a tomato growing business. He became involved with football once again, working with the island team, and was great friends with Latics legend Bobby Johnstone.

SATURDAY 28TH JANUARY 1967

Having beaten Notts County and Grantham in previous rounds, Athletic took on Wolverhampton Wanderers in the third round of the FA Cup at Boundary Park. Manager Jimmy McIlroy had boldly blooded teenagers Ronnie Blair, Ian Wood and Les Chapman for the game and it seemed to have paid off as the Latics were two goals up after the regulation 90 minutes. Keith Bebbington got both goals in front of 24, 968 enthusiastic supporters. Miraculously, Wolves got two goals in the dying minutes of added injury time to force a draw. The Latics fans were left dumbfounded as they could not believe what had just happened. Wolves won the replay 4-1.

TUESDAY 29TH JANUARY 1929

Centre-forward Stewart Littlewood signed from Port Vale for a fee of £1,300 and despite only playing half the season, he still finished the campaign as the club's leading goalscorer with 12 goals.

SATURDAY 29TH JANUARY 1977

An administration error meant a change of venue for the Latics FA Cup fourth round tie with Northwich Victoria. The non-league side had drawn Athletic at home but such was the demand to see the game, they sold more tickets than their Drillfield ground could hold and were forced to switch the game to Maine Road, Manchester. Athletic won 3-1. Two goals from Vic Halom, and one from Carl Valentine, were enough to see off the non-league team in front of 28,635 spectators.

FRIDAY 30th JANUARY 1959

Ace goal poacher Roger Palmer was born in Manchester. Palmer wrote himself into the history books by becoming the all-time aggregate scorer for Athletic. He was bought by Jimmy Frizzell for £70,000 as a replacement for Simon Stainrod who had recently been sold for £250,000 to Queens Park Rangers, one of the best transfer dealings ever by the club. When new manager Joe Royle took over from Frizzell he said of Palmer, "Roger has only one trick, he puts the ball into the back of the net". He broke Eric Gemmell's all-time scoring record with a spectacular diving header against Ipswich Town. It was his 110th goal and shattered Gemmell's 35-year-old record. Gemmell was there to witness the feat. It is a testament to his popularity that even today the fans still sing the chant of "Ooh, Roger Palmer".

SATURDAY 31st JANUARY 1981

In a struggling season, and with Athletic at the wrong end of the Second Division, the Latics won at Cardiff City with goals from Martin Nuttall and Roger Palmer. The result put the Latics in 17th place in the league.

WEDNESDAY 31st JANUARY 1990

Urged on by 18,862 ecstatic supporters, Athletic kept up their record of scoring in every round of the League Cup. First Division Southampton were the visitors for a replay – secured with an equaliser in the dying seconds of the first game at the Dell. Andy Ritchie got an early goal and Mike Milligan snatched a crucial second goal to give the Saints a mountain to climb. Athletic held on to record their 30th match unbeaten at home, breaking a record dating back to 1923/24. Saints manager Chris Nicholl commented, "Oldham are a good side and have given us as many problems as some First Division teams. Good luck to them".

FRIDAY 31st JANUARY 2003

Pushing for promotion from the Second Division, Athletic maintained the best away league record in Britain with a 1-1 draw at Ninian Park. After one of the biggest league games for several season, the result left the Latics in third place just one point ahead of the Bluebirds. Trailing 1-0 at the half, and watched by more than 12,500 fans, David Eyres smashed a deserved equaliser in the 87th minute which silenced the majority of the watching crowd.

OLDHAM ATHLETIC
On This Day

FEBRUARY

SUNDAY 1st FEBRUARY 1959

Simon Stainrod was born in Sheffield. Athletic paid a club record fee of £60,000 to Sheffield United when they signed him in 1979 but it was to be a good investment as he was later sold to Queens Park Rangers for £250,000. His style was not popular with all his clubs but he warmed the hearts of the Oldham faithful and was probably the father of flamboyant goalscoring celebrations. In his 69 league games for Athletic he netted 21 goals, most of them being spectacular.

MONDAY 2nd FEBRUARY 1920

Future Latics player and manager George Hardwick was born in Saltburn. He joined Athletic in 1950 for a fee of £15,000. In the post-war years he was captain of England and eventually became the youngest-ever manager of the club. He led the Latics to the Third Division (North) championship. A former Middlesbrough and Chelsea player, Hardwick was a natural leader who made 190 league appearances, chipping in with 14 goals.

SATURDAY 2nd FEBRUARY 1963

Table-topping Athletic entertained nearby neighbours Rochdale in the Fourth Division, and remained on course for promotion as they sent them home stinging after a 5-1 mauling. Bert Lister and Colin Whittaker got two goals apiece and Johnny Colquhoun got the other in a game which showed no mercy on handily placed Dale.

SATURDAY 2nd FEBRUARY 1991

A trip to Oxford United resulted in what was a rare defeat in 1990/91: a 5-1 hammering. It was the club's heaviest defeat of the season but they could take some consolation in the fact they were still the top goalscorers in the entire Football League with 55 goals to their credit.

SATURDAY 2nd FEBRUARY 2008

Athletic visited the Liberty Stadium looking for their tenth consecutive away game without defeat but went down 2-1 to Swansea City. With the home side pushing for promotion to the Championship, the game was watched by a decent gate of 12,458, who saw Craig Davies score a penalty for the only Latics goal. The result left Athletic in 14th place in League One.

FRIDAY 3rd FEBRUARY 1911

Centre-forward Tommy Davis was born in Dublin. Homesick, he walked out on French club FC de Metz to join Oldham in June 1936 – after failing to settle in France after moving across the English Channel in 1935. For breaking his contract he was suspended by the FA for three months, so couldn't make his debut until October. He scored in his first game at home to former club New Brighton: a 6-0 win. Davis scored 55 first team goals in 79 appearances before being transferred to Tranmere Rovers. He still holds Athletic's individual record for the most goals in a season, after he hit the net 33 times in the 1936-37 campaign.

TUESDAY 3rd FEBRUARY 1953

Goalkeeper Chris Ogden was born in Oldham. Ogden took over from the famous Latics keeper Harry Dowd when he was just 18 years old. He struggled in his first season by letting in 16 goals in his first six games before making the keeper's spot his own. Son of Fred Ogden, he appeared 143 times for Athletic.

TUESDAY 3rd FEBRUARY 2004

A group of American-based expatriate British businessmen bought the club, forming a new company Oldham Athletic (2004) Association Football Club Ltd, thus ensuring that Oldham would survive. After some months in administration the club had only hours to live before Danny Gazal, Simon Blitz and Simon Corney (aka the 'Three Amigos') took ownership and agreed with the administrators to fund the £250,000 monthly figure required by the club. They immediately agreed to sell 3% of the club for £200,000 to Trust Oldham, the supporters' trust.

SATURDAY 4th FEBRUARY 1989

Jon Hallworth made his debut in the home match against Watford. The keeper joined a team that had not won for 15 matches and the Hornets were riding high in second place in the Second Division, as well as having just disposed of First Division Derby County in the fourth round of the FA Cup. However, two goals from Andy Ritchie and one from Denis Irwin sealed a welcome 3-1 win for Athletic which kicked off a ten-match unbeaten run.

WEDNESDAY 5th FEBRUARY 1908

After a 0-0 draw at Boundary Park the Latics were at Goodison Park for an FA Cup second round replay. Over 25,000 supporters were at each of the matches but it was the Everton fans who went home happy after an emphatic 6-1 drubbing of Athletic. Alex Whaites got the consolation goal for Oldham on a miserable day for the Latics followers who made the trip across Lancashire.

TUESDAY 5th FEBRUARY 1991

Earl Barrett made his international England debut in the England 'B' side in the match against Wales 'B' played in Swansea. He put in an outstanding performance which put pressure on senior England players Des Walker and Mark Wright. England boss Graham Taylor watched the game and was very impressed with his performance.

SATURDAY 5th FEBRUARY 1994

Southampton were at Boundary Park for a Premiership game. Athletic desperately needed the points as they were battling to move away from the relegation zone – and the home fans were delighted as they ground out a 2-1 win with goals from midfielder Paul Bernard and powerful striker Sean McCarthy.

SATURDAY 6th FEBRUARY 1937

Athletic had a great chance to enhance their own promotion chances in the Third Division North title race, as leaders Stockport County came to town. The derby was watched by over 23,000 fanatical supporters but the home fans were disappointed as they saw their team lose 2-0 to the eventual champions. The result demoralised the team and sent them on a fall from grace which effectively became the turning point of the season. The best the team could achieve was fourth spot, not promotion, as was earlier expected.

THURSDAY 6th FEBRUARY 1947

John Hurst was born in Blackpool. Hurst signed from Everton in 1976 and was an experienced defender who never played out of the top two divisions. The England under-23 player made 170 appearances for the Latics and scored two goals. He won honours with Everton as Football League champions and FA Cup finalists.

WEDNESDAY 6TH FEBRUARY 1991

The inclusion of Denis Irwin in the Republic of Ireland's friendly international game against Wales in Wrexham handed Athletic a windfall of £75,000 which was part of the deal that took him to Manchester United in a £650,000 move the previous summer.

MONDAY 7TH FEBRUARY 1938

Goalkeeper John Hardie was born in Edinburgh. Although he played only 17 matches for the Latics he was a member of the famous Bobby Johnstone-era team competing with Jimmy Rollo for the number one shirt. Signed from Hibernian in 1960 he was later sold to Chester.

SUNDAY 8TH FEBRUARY 2004

"Celebration Sunday" was the day when the new owners of Oldham Athletic threw open the gates for free and a capacity gate of 13,007 watched the Latics completely demolish Grimsby Town. A Scott Vernon hat-trick and goals from Adam Griffin and Jermain Johnston ensured that the Latics would have a day to remember as they raced into a 5-0 half-time lead. Five minutes from time, substitute Calvin Zola smashed in the sixth goal to crown a comprehensive 6-0 drubbing of the hapless Mariners.

SATURDAY 9TH FEBRUARY 1963

Goalkeeper William Matthews died in Oldham. He was the son of famous amateur keeper Howard Matthews. He played 344 times in the league for Athletic and continued playing at Halifax into his 45th year as one of the oldest league players of all time.

MONDAY 10TH FEBRUARY 1913

Liverpool were the visitors to Boundary Park on this day for a First Division game. Two goals from Arthur Gee and one from Gilbert Kemp won the game 3-1 for Athletic.

SATURDAY 10TH FEBRUARY 1934

Struggling Manchester United were at Boundary Park for a Second Division game. Thomas Reid, Peter Burke and Clifton Chadwick scored the Latics goals in a 3-2 thriller which left the Red Devils next to the bottom of the league. A crowd of 24,480 watched the game.

SATURDAY 10TH FEBRUARY 2007

Table-topping Athletic were at League One promotion rivals Swansea City. Paul Warne got the only goal which cemented the Latics in top spot in a game watched by 9,880 fans.

WEDNESDAY 11TH FEBRUARY 1920

Goalkeeper George Burnett was born in Birkenhead. He joined Athletic from Everton for £7,500 as cover for Fred Ogden and went on to make 105 appearances for the Boundary Park team. He took crosses well and he only conceded five goals in his first ten games. He was in goal when George Hardwick's team won their first ever championship with a 0-0 draw at Bradford City. George died in Birkenhead on 29th April 1985.

SATURDAY 11TH FEBRUARY 1967

A 2-1 loss at Bristol Rovers was the game that saw Les Chapman make his debut for Athletic. Ian Towers scored the only Athletic goal in a match that left Athletic in seventh place in the Third Division table.

TUESDAY 11TH FEBRUARY 1997

Athletic manager Graeme Sharp had his contract terminated along with his assistant Colin Harvey. The Latics were struggling at the bottom of the First Division. Neil Warnock was brought in to stop the rot. However, it was a case of too-little too-late as come the end of the season the Latics were relegated.

SATURDAY 12TH FEBRUARY 1927

The Latics went to Blundell Park to face Grimsby Town for this Second Division game. Maurice Wellock got four goals and Horace Barnes netted another in a convincing 5-2 victory over the Mariners.

SATURDAY 12TH FEBRUARY 1949

Athletic ran riot over Darlington in a Third Division (North) game. With Athletic struggling and the Quakers pushing for promotion, the result was a pleasant surprise for the 15,034 supporters who turned up at Boundary Park. Frank Tomlinson, Harry Stock, Eric Gemmell (2), William Jessop and Ray Haddington 2 (1 pen) got the markers on the day in a 7-1 win.

SATURDAY 13TH FEBRUARY 1932

Promotion-chasing Leeds United visited Boundary Park for a Second Division fixture. A goal from William Johnstone and a penalty from James Dyson secured the win that knocked Leeds off top spot and left them one point behind new leaders Wolverhampton Wanderers. Only 6,496 supporters bothered to turn up to see the table-toppers.

SATURDAY 13TH FEBRUARY 1937

With a paltry 3,539 supporters inside Millmoor, the stay-aways missed a cracking 4-4 draw between Rotherham United and Oldham. A Tommy Davis hat-trick and a goal by Patrick Robbins did enough to secure a hard-earned point.

SUNDAY 14TH FEBRUARY 1897

Centre-half Seth King was born in Penistone. He joined Athletic in May 1929 for a fee of £400. He was a tough-tackling player who didn't miss many games but after 96 appearances his contract was cancelled in February 1932.

WEDNESDAY 14TH FEBRUARY 1990

One of the most memorable nights in the history of Oldham Athletic. A confident West Ham team visited Boundary Park for the first leg of the League Cup semi-final. Manager Lou Macari had stated that his team had an advantage being at home, playing in front of the West Ham fans for the second leg – but he failed to realise that Athletic were in rampant form and thrashing all-comers in their march towards two possible Wembley appearances in what was becoming known amongst Latics fans as the "pinch-me" season. The form book went out of the window as the Latics tore apart a frail sweeper system that was employed by the Hammers. Manager Joe Royle pulled Ian Marshall out of defence and used him as a fifth forward. And it paid off, as the Latics went goal crazy in front of 19,263 home fans, hitting the Hammers for six without reply. Neil Adams, Andy Ritchie (2), Earl Barrett, Rick Holden and Roger Palmer got the goals in the biggest-ever semi-final win in the history of the League Cup competition. Oldham were all but assured a place in the League Cup Final after this game, which is now known as the 'St Valentine's Day Massacre.'

SATURDAY 15TH FEBRUARY 2003

An amazing away record continued for Athletic with a 2-1 win at Stockport County in the Second Division. Paul Murray put the Latics ahead in the ninth minute, only for County to equalise. However, another late winner from David Eyres in the 89th minute sealed the victory. Over 3,000 Athletic fans made the short trip to Edgeley Park to watch the run continue – it was now ten and a half months since Oldham had lost on their travels!

WEDNESDAY 15TH FEBRUARY 2006

A convincing second-half display from Athletic saw Ritchie Wellens, Richard Butcher and Luke Beckett all find the net in the space of 29 minutes against a Nottingham Forest team which had picked up just one win in ten League One games. Angry Forest fans called for manager Gary Megson to be sacked after the abysmal performance. The 3-0 win was revenge for a same-scoreline drubbing that Athletic had suffered the previous month at the City Ground when Forest had looked a completely different team.

TUESDAY 16TH FEBRUARY 1937

Popular manager Jimmy Frizzell was born in Greenock. He signed for Athletic for a fee of £1,500 in 1960 and remained at Boundary Park until 1982. He was an accomplished player and exceptional manager who made 350 appearances as a player and netted 58 goals. He went on to become first team coach in 1968 – after Jimmy McIlroy departed – caretaker manager in 1969 and manager in 1970. Frizzell was an inside-forward, but was equally at home anywhere on the field. His brave style made him leading goalscorer in 1961/62 (24) and 1964/65 (11) but he dropped to wing-half, then later to a full-back. He led Athletic to promotion in 1962/63 and in his first season as manager he scooped a £70,000 pay-off as his team monopolised the new Ford Sporting League. The funding built the new Broadway stand at Boundary Park. Frizzell also led the team to promotion to the Second Division, a position they held for a record spell and he guided the Latics to respectability before being sensationally sacked as the second-longest-serving manager in the Football League. He was held in such high esteem that he was nicknamed 'Sir' Jimmy Frizzell by the fans.

TUESDAY 16TH FEBRUARY 1985

The Second Division's bottom club Cardiff City shocked the Latics with a 1-0 home loss in a game to forget for Oldham fans.

SATURDAY 17TH FEBRUARY 1990

Everton had appeared in four of the last six FA Cup finals and they brought their team to Boundary Park looking to progress once more against Second Division opposition in this quarter-final game. The Toffees looked to be on course as they took a 2-0 half-time lead with goals from Graeme Sharp and Tony Cottee. Another capacity gate of 19,320 roared on the Latics for a second-half fightback and they watched their heroes pull back a goal in the 60th minute from an Andy Ritchie penalty after Southall was adjudged to have impeded Roger Palmer. Palmer got the all-important equaliser in the 66th minute when he headed home his fourth goal in four games.

SUNDAY 18TH FEBRUARY 1962

England under-21 player John Ryan was born in Failsworth. He played 108 games for the Latics in two spells, contributing eight goals along the way. Ryan moved to Newcastle in 1983 for a fairly sizeable fee of £225,000 – but incoming manager Jack Charlton moved him on within two months to Sheffield Wednesday. He left Hillsborough to return to Oldham for his second spell in 1985. A double fracture of his left leg at Tranmere Rovers in 1986 proved to be too much to recover from – although the injury remained undiscovered until his next game, at home to Derby County he was substituted at half-time, and sadly he never played again.

SATURDAY 19TH FEBRUARY 1921

Arsenal entertained Athletic at Highbury for a First Division fixture. The match was watched by over 18,000 supporters, who saw the visitors come away with a well-earned point after a 2-2 draw. Reuben Butler got both Athletic's goals, one a penalty.

SATURDAY 19TH FEBRUARY 1994

A 15,685 crowd packed into Boundary Park to witness this FA Cup fifth round game against Barnsley. Andy Ritchie got the only goal of the game to send the Latics into the quarter-finals.

FRIDAY 20th FEBRUARY 1885

Bolden, near Sunderland, was the birthplace of George Wall. The English international winger spent two years at Athletic just after World War I, then playing as a veteran, and was almost an ever-present. He turned out 74 times in the league and notched 12 goals.

SUNDAY 20th FEBRUARY 1944

Wing-half Ken Knighton was born in Mexborough. Knighton made just 46 league appearances and scored five goals in his one-year stay at Boundary Park. He arrived from Wolverhampton Wanderers in 1966 for £12,000 and was sold to Preston North End for £35,000 after proving his ability both as a defender and an attacker.

MONDAY 20th FEBRUARY 1967

Mike Milligan was born in Moss Side, Manchester. He made a total of 331 appearances for the club where he started his career after they received a grant from the European Social Fund. Milligan was a hard-working midfielder who went on to captain the side, making 60 appearances in 1989/90. He scored 26 times and was voted supporters' 'Player of the Year' in May 1990. Everton acquired his services in a £1m move – the club's first player to move for that amount. He returned for a second spell at Boundary Park a year later, for a record fee of £600,000, but after the Latics got relegated in 1994 he moved on to Norwich City for a fee of £850,000.

FRIDAY 21st FEBRUARY 1969

Liverpool was the birthplace of Nick Henry. He arrived at Boundary Park as a 15-year-old and asked for a trial with Athletic, who were struggling at the wrong end of the Second Division. Henry was sent on loan to play in the Swedish First Division and then established himself as a first teamer in the 1988/89 season when he became a fans' favourite for his dogged determination and great work-rate. His first goal for Athletic came against Arsenal in a shock 3-1 defeat for the Gunners in the fourth round of the League Cup. It was a 30-yard screamer! He formed a great midfield partnership with Mike Milligan and went on to make 328 appearances for the Latics, scoring 22 goals, before being transferred to Sheffield United for £500,000 in a deal which brought Doug Hodgson to Boundary Park.

SATURDAY 21st FEBRUARY 1970

Oldham Athletic visited Bootham Crescent, home of York City. Jimmy Fryatt, who was making his debut, had recently signed from Blackburn Rovers after languishing in their reserve team. Unfortunately, he couldn't make it a goalscoring first performance as the result was a 0-0 draw.

WEDNESDAY 21st FEBRUARY 1990

The cup saga continued with an FA Cup quarter-final replay at Everton. After a 2-2 draw at Boundary Park this fixture went into marathon mode ending 0-0. The game could not be concluded in extra time. Athletic silenced most of the 36,663 attendees when Everton old boy Ian Marshall headed the Latics in front, although Oldham's travelling supporters gave a tremendous roar of approval. The game was a niggling and bruising affair. Four Everton players had been booked in the first game at Oldham and another five were cautioned, as well as a sending-off for Norman Whiteside. Everton's blushes were saved after they were awarded a penalty after Jon Hallworth collided with Graeme Sharp. Kevin Sheedy stepped up to convert from the spot. A second replay was now required!

FRIDAY 22nd FEBRUARY 1952

Future Latics player Ian Robins was born in Bury. He made his debut at the ripe age of 17 years but from 1967-71 he spent most of his time in the reserves. New manager Jimmy Frizzell gave him his chance and he came on in leaps and bounds after being switched from the wing to a midfield role. His 46 goals in 239 appearances contributed to a successful spell for him at Oldham. He was the first Athletic apprentice to be selected for the England youth team trials in 1969 and he eventually transferred to Bury for a fee of £25,000 in July 1977.

SATURDAY 22nd FEBRUARY 2003

Ex-Latics favourite Billy Dearden brought his Notts County team to Boundary Park for a Second Division fixture and left with a point from a 1-1 draw. Striker Wayne Andrews got the Latics goal in the 44th minute which left Athletic in fourth spot with 59 points, an equal total with third-placed Cardiff City.

LATICS FAVOURITE IAN MARSHALL WAS ON TARGET AGAINST EVERTON IN THE CUP IN FEBRUARY 1990

FRIDAY 23RD FEBRUARY 1945

Frank Womack took over as new manager at Boundary Park for the wartime competitions. He was renowned as a 'doctor' to football clubs and had previously managed at Torquay United, Grimsby Town, Leicester City and Notts County. He was not afraid of giving youth a chance and put out a new team every week to retain interest for the fans.

SATURDAY 23RD FEBRUARY 1974

A crowd of 9,145 turned out at Boundary Park to watch Alan Groves make his debut against Aldershot. A goal from the penalty spot by Maurice Whittle and another from 'Grovesey' gave the Latics a 2-0 victory.

SATURDAY 24TH FEBRUARY 1990

Ipswich Town were the visitors for this Division Two game. Athletic put in a workmanlike performance to gain a convincing 4-1 victory. Ian Marshall got two goals, Roger Palmer and Denis Irwin completed the scoring.

SATURDAY 24TH FEBRUARY 2007

Different needs were required in this League One game with Athletic pushing for promotion and AFC Bournemouth fighting against relegation. The Cherries raced into a 2-0 lead but a penalty from Andy Liddell made it 2-1 after Chris Porter had been brought down. It wasn't enough to stop Athletic falling to their third consecutive defeat. To make matters worse, Ben Turner was sent off in injury time.

TUESDAY 25TH FEBRUARY 1992

Earl Barrett joined Aston Villa for £1.7m in a record-breaking deal. He had joined Athletic from Manchester City in 1987 for a fee of £35,000. Not a bad mark-up after some sterling service.

SATURDAY 25TH FEBRUARY 1995

Athletic put up a good show when Sheffield United came to town for this League One match. In a finely balanced game, two goals from Nicky Banger and another from Andy Ritchie gave the home side a share of the spoils in a 3-3 game watched by almost 10,000 fans.

SATURDAY 25TH FEBRUARY 2006

A 1-0 victory over Tranmere Rovers was enough to keep the Latics on track with their promotion play-off aspirations. Manager Ronnie Moore watched his side earn their tenth point out of the last twelve when a long-range free-kick from Ritchie Wellens hit the back of the net. Old boys Calvin Zola and Delroy Facey came up against their former employers but couldn't do anything to save the game.

WEDNESDAY 26TH FEBRUARY 1913

Athletic visited Old Trafford for a fifth round FA Cup replay with Manchester United. Four days earlier the teams had drawn 0-0 at Boundary Park. The Latics put in a sterling performance to spring the shock result of the competition with a 2-1 victory. Gee and Toward did the damage with the Oldham goals. In an unexpected move after the match, Latics centre-half George Hunter was immediately sold to Chelsea with no reason being explained for his departure!

TUESDAY 26TH FEBRUARY 1952

Padiham was the birthplace of David Holt on this day. Holt cost Athletic a record fee of £25,000 (plus Tony Bailey) when he signed from Bury in 1974. A solid defender, who moved to the full-back position to partner Ian Wood, he made his debut against Sheffield Wednesday on 14th December 1974 and played 142 league games, scoring 11 goals.

WEDNESDAY 26TH FEBRUARY 1964

Latics legend David Eyres was born in Liverpool. Eyres was the ultimate professional and gentleman who left fond memories at all the clubs he played for. Starting late in football at the age of 25, he arrived at Athletic from Preston North End in 2000 on a free transfer under the reign of manager Andy Ritchie. In his first full season he was the club's leading goalscorer with 12, had most appearances with 47 – plus five as substitute – and also won the 'Player of the Year' award. In 2003, the evergreen player signed a contract to keep him playing until his 40th birthday. Eyres was appointed assistant caretaker manager to John Sheridan after the Chris Moore fiasco moved on Iain Dowie. He was also joint caretaker manager with Tony Philliskirk after Brian Talbot had been dismissed from Boundary Park. Eyres is a true Latics legend who scored 41 goals in 231 appearances.

MONDAY 26TH FEBRUARY 1979

Leicester City visited Athletic in the fourth round of the FA Cup as 11,972 fans watched. An Alan Young hat-trick was just the ticket as the home side put in a rousing performance to reach the fifth round against Tottenham Hotspur. Unfortunately, fixtures were such that they had to take on Spurs just two days after this game.

SATURDAY 27TH FEBRUARY 1982

Athletic went to Kenilworth Road to take on Luton Town in a Second Division game. The Latics were highly fancied for promotion but a 2-0 loss to the Hatters was a bitter pill to swallow as it started a run of nine games without a win. Injuries and suspensions added to the misery and they all began to take their toll. Luton went on to be champions of the division.

WEDNESDAY 28TH FEBRUARY 1979

Just two days after seeing off Leicester City in the FA Cup, the Latics entertained Tottenham Hotspur in the fifth round of the competition. Tired legs must have been a major contributing factor to the Latics falling to a single goal loss in front of 16,097 supporters. The result meant that Athletic missed out on a glamorous fixture against Manchester United in the next round.

SATURDAY 29TH FEBRUARY 1908

Bottom club Chesterfield were the visitors for a Second Division game. Around 6,000 people watch the Latics hammer the Spireites 4-0. James Hamilton scored a penalty while Frank Newton and John Hesham (2) completed the scoring. The result left Athletic in third place.

SATURDAY 29TH FEBRUARY 1936

Athletic visited the Tower Ground to take on the side bottom of the Third Division (North). There was to be no upset as New Brighton were convincingly beaten 3-1 by goals from William Walsh and Arthur Buckley (2) in front of 1,490 spectators.

OLDHAM ATHLETIC
On This Day

MARCH

WEDNESDAY 1st MARCH 1939

Tommy Bryceland was born in Greenock. Signed from Norwich City, Bryceland was an influential midfielder who helped Athletic to promotion in the 1970/71 season. The Latics supporters also voted him Player of the Year in the same campaign. He played 67 games for Oldham and scored 10 goals.

THURSDAY 1st MARCH 1973

Athletic appointed Tony Smyth as club secretary but he stepped down just two days later due to ill health. The resignation made him the shortest-serving secretary in Football League history.

SATURDAY 1st MARCH 2003

With the only unbeaten away record in the league, Athletic went to struggling Mansfield Town for a League One match. They won 1-0 with a controversial penalty in the 88th minute which was converted by Fitz Hall. The match will be remembered more for the refereeing decisions – three players were sent off and eight were booked. David Eyres was dismissed in the 34th minute for violent conduct.

SATURDAY 1st MARCH 2008

Athletic claimed their first win at Vale Park in 12 years with a 3-0 score which left Port Vale needing a miracle to escape relegation from League One. The goals were scored by Jordan Robertson, Neal Eardley and Matty Wolfenden. Vale were relegated with 38 points at the end of the season.

SATURDAY 2nd MARCH 1901

Jimmy Naylor was born in High Crompton. He was an England trialist who had two spells at the club. One of the best-ever locally produced players, he scored six goals in 249 outings. After finding fame in the First Division with Huddersfield Town and Newcastle United he returned to his roots and helped steer Athletic clear of relegation in the 1932/33 season. Jimmy died on 31st August 1983 in Shaw.

SATURDAY 2nd MARCH 1991

Athletic went to Brighton for a Third Division game and emerged as 2-1 victors. Andy Ritchie got both of Athletic's goals, his second one was a cracker and well worthy of the goal of the season accolade.

SATURDAY 3rd MARCH 1928

A Second Division game at South Shields resulted in a fine 3-0 away win for the Latics. The north-east club were bottom of the league. A goal from John King and two from Albert Pynegar sealed the victory.

SATURDAY 3rd MARCH 2007

Promotion-chasing Athletic visited Brunton Park to take on League One challengers Carlisle United. Having lost their last four games they looked well on course to end their dismal run after Chris Taylor had scored his first-ever senior goal for the Latics. He was so excited at having notched his first goal in 51 games that he got booked for over celebrating. Substitute Derek Holmes spoiled the party by equalising for the Cumbrians with three minutes of the game remaining. The draw left Athletic in fifth place and the goal inspired a production of 'I saw Taylor score' T-shirts.

SATURDAY 4th MARCH 1957

Jimmy Faye died in Southport. He joined Athletic in May 1905 when they played at Hudson Fold. His first contract paid him 30 shillings a week with travelling expenses, but the way that Athletic made such a meteoric rise in those days meant that he was being paid £4 per week within just three years. He was transferred to Bolton Wanderers in 1911 for a fee of £750 after scoring 40 goals in 175 games for the Latics.

FRIDAY 4th MARCH 1988

Defender Andy Linighan was sold to Norwich City for £350,000. He had joined Athletic in a £55,000 deal from Leeds United in January 1986.

TUESDAY 4th MARCH 2003

Bristol City inflicted the first away Division Two defeat of the season on Athletic with a 2-0 victory. A 17-game unbeaten away record had been a remarkable feat but the Latics succumbed in a whimper to a Bristol team who had just hit a purple patch. There were 11,194 supporters there to witness the result.

SATURDAY 5TH MARCH 1932

A home game in the Second Division against Chesterfield resulted in a 6-1 win for Athletic. Both teams were struggling in the league but a hat-trick from John Pears and goals from Matt Gray, William Johnstone and Harold Brown sealed a convincing victory over the Spireites.

TUESDAY 5TH MARCH 1974

Cambridge United came to Boundary Park with the Latics on course for promotion from the Third Division and having won their last six league games. The Us were like lambs to the slaughter as Athletic ran up a 6-1 scoreline with goals from Maurice Whittle (pen), Keith Hicks, George McVitie, Colin Garwood, Alan Groves and George Jones. Athletic finished the season as champions.

SUNDAY 6TH MARCH 1938

Popular centre-forward – and the record holder of most goals in a season – Tommy Davis returned to Boundary Park with his new team Tranmere Rovers for a Third Division (North) match. In a testament to his popularity, the gate was almost doubled from the previous home game to 21,548. Two goals from Matt Gray earned Athletic a 2-1 win while the Latics defence did enough to stop Davis from scoring.

SUNDAY 6TH MARCH 1949

Former Manchester United and Scottish international team captain Martin Buchan was born in Aberdeen. Buchan helped Athletic to survival in the 1983/84 season but retired from the game with a persistent thigh injury after only four games the following season. He made 28 appearances for Athletic.

WEDNESDAY 7TH MARCH 1990

Wembley became a reality for Athletic after they went to West Ham United for the second leg of the League Cup semi-final. With a 6-0 record win under their belt from the first leg all they had to do was play safe. They lost 3-0 on the night, a result which brought some pride back for the Hammers but the score was insignificant as Athletic had booked their first-ever game at Wembley, the first major final in the club's history.

SATURDAY 8TH MARCH 1913

Athletic had to travel to Goodison Park for a sixth round FA Cup game with Everton. Arthur Gee somehow sneaked the only goal of the contest to not only shock the Toffees but also to send the Latics on their way to the semi-finals for the first time in their history.

MONDAY 8TH MARCH 1954

Ace goal poacher Rodger Wylde was born in Sheffield. Wylde was signed from Sheffield Wednesday in 1980 for a fee of £75,000 and he soon became a crowd favourite at Boundary Park. His return of 51 goals in 113 appearances over three seasons made him the club's leading scorer in all three campaigns. He was bought to replace Vic Halom and made an immediate impact. On leaving Oldham, he moved to Sporting Lisbon and then returned to England when Sunderland signed him in 1984.

SATURDAY 8TH MARCH 2003

A 2-0 win over Colchester United was only the Latics' second Division Two win in nine matches but their results on the road meant that Athletic were still on course for an automatic promotion place. Early goals from John Eyre and David Eyres were enough to kill off any threat that Colchester could muster.

SUNDAY 9TH MARCH 1941

Prolific goalscorer Andy Lochhead was born in Glasgow and was an influential player and particularly good in the air. Lochhead, remarkably, only scored 10 goals for the Latics in his one-year and 45 league game spell. He was a member of the 1973/74 Third Division championship side and went on to join the coaching staff after Bobby Collins moved on to Huddersfield Town.

SATURDAY 9TH MARCH 1991

Goals from Andy Ritchie and Neil Redfearn were enough to dispel any threat from Bristol Rovers at Boundary Park. The 2-0 win, witnessed by 12,775 fans, took Athletic back to the top of the Second Division league table.

SATURDAY 10TH MARCH 1990

The fifth round marathon FA Cup game continued at Boundary Park. After two draws and extra time, Everton came to Oldham for the second time to try to settle the game once and for all. Tony Cottee put the visitors ahead in the 12th minute but Roger Palmer equalised in the 33rd minute after a poor back pass by Neil McDonald – a future Oldham player – to Neville Southall was intercepted and punished.

True to form this game went to extra time and was settled by a penalty after Marshall had been brought down. Marshall took the kick himself to knock out the team who had previously rejected him. Athletic now faced First Division leaders Aston Villa in the quarter-finals for their first appearance at this stage in 77 years.

SATURDAY 11TH MARCH 1961

Runaway Fourth Division leaders Peterborough United visited Athletic in their first-ever season in the Football League. A total of 27,888 people – the highest gate for seven years – crammed into Boundary Park to witness the event and they were treated to a game that would have graced the First Division. The Posh took the lead through Ripley with a 30-yard scorcher but a penalty in the 75th minute, scored by Ken Branagan, meant that the teams would share the points in a pulsating match that both teams deserved something out of.

FRIDAY 11TH MARCH 1966

Chairman Ken Bates appointed Jimmy McIlroy as team manager in late January on a five-year deal. He was then made player-manager making his Athletic debut in a 2-0 win at Southend United. Gordon Hurst had previously been promised full backing from Mr Bates and it came as quite a shock when McIlroy arrived on the scene. The new manager took over a club who were at the wrong end of the Third Division but still managed to finish in 20th place, just above the relegation places.

FRIDAY 11th MARCH 1988

Everton defender Ian Marshall joined Athletic on loan but manager Joe Royle made the deal a permanent one a couple of weeks later. He was to become a superb defender, as well as an accomplished striker, at Oldham and he went back to 'haunt' Everton on many occasions.

TUESDAY 12th MARCH 1974

York City came to Boundary Park and 15,871 people showed up to watch them play a Third Division game. The Latics were looking for their tenth consecutive league win and they did not disappoint the crowd. Two goals from Maurice Whittle, one a penalty, were enough to see off York 2-1 and, in the process, create a new piece of history for the club.

SATURDAY 12th MARCH 1988

Andy Rhodes and Ian Marshall both made their debuts for Athletic in the home Third Division game against Swindon Town. In a match where Frankie Bunn scored, Andy Ritchie got two – one a penalty – and Roger Palmer scored his 99th goal for the Latics, they went on to win the thriller by a 4-3 scoreline.

TUESDAY 12th MARCH 1991

Roger Palmer hit his 150th goal for Athletic in a 2-2 draw at Swindon Town. His striking partner Andy Ritchie was the other Latics marksman in the Second Division game.

TUESDAY 13th MARCH 1945

Manager Andrew Wilson died. He served from July 1927 until July 1932 and his 1929/30 team finished in third place in the Second Division. His famous players were: Jack Hacking, Teddy Ivill, Billy Porter, Les Adlam, Seth King, Ted Goodier, Fred Worrall, Jimmy Dyson, Lawrie Cumming, Stewart Littlewood, Matt Gray and Bill Hasson – all household names at the time.

SATURDAY 14th MARCH 1953

Table-topping Athletic entertained Carlisle United in a Third Division (North) fixture, but were shocked as the Cumbrians went home with a 4-2 victory. Ken Brierley and Bill Ormond got the Latics goals in a pulsating game which was attended by more than 20,000 enthusiastic fans.

WEDNESDAY 14TH MARCH 1990

First Division leaders Aston Villa were the next big team to visit Oldham for a cup game in a remarkable season. All the previous opponents had gone home with their tails between their legs. Could Athletic do it again?

Another capacity gate of 19,490 were in attendance to witness that they could! Joe Royle's young team just kept getting better as each big name came along. They brushed aside any threat from their illustrious visitors and amazingly beat them by a 3-0 scoreline. It was becoming a Roy of the Rovers performance now. Rick Holden opened the scoring in the 38th minute and an own goal put the Latics two ahead. Neil Redfearn completed the demolition.

Villa boss Graham Taylor graciously admitted, "They are so direct. They get the ball into the box quickly – more than any First Division team we have met. They'll give any team in the land problems". The win set up a semi-final game with Manchester United and the chance for Athletic to visit Wembley twice in the same season in both domestic finals.

SATURDAY 15TH MARCH 2003

Queens Park Rangers came to Boundary Park for a Division Two promotion battle. Future Latics keeper Chris Day was in goal for the visitors but it was Les Pogliacomi who won the honours with a great display to keep the Rangers attack at bay. It was his 16th clean sheet in 37 games and the 0-0 draw left both teams still in with a shout of promotion.

SATURDAY 16TH MARCH 1974

A huge contingent of Latics followers made the trip to Derbyshire to take on high-flying Chesterfield. Athletic were on an all-time record run of ten consecutive wins in the Third Division and were looking for their eleventh, but it wasn't to be. The Spireites won 1-0 and the travelling faithful had a miserable, long and dangerous trip home through the snow-filled Pennines.

WEDNESDAY 17TH MARCH 1915

A rearranged league game saw the top two teams in Division One meet at Everton. Oldham took the lead through Oliver Tummon and then Arthur Gee put them two up with a neat header. The Toffees pulled one back but the Latics scored again through Arthur Gee. Tummon got his second before two more Everton goals made it a tense finish in front of around 8,000 fans. Athletic held on to win 4-3 but the Liverpool outfit had the last laugh by winning the League championship by one point.

SATURDAY 17TH MARCH 1923

A Bill Blyth strike, and an own goal by Reg Freeman, gave Arsenal a 2-0 win against Athletic in front of 30,000 spectators. The result left Athletic firmly rooted at the bottom of the First Division with just one away win to their credit.

WEDNESDAY 18TH MARCH 1942

Athletic winger Reggie Blore was born in Wrexham. Ginger-top Blore was a big hit with the Latics faithful and he scored 19 goals in 181 league appearances. He was a member of the Southport team that got slammed 11-0 by Athletic on their record-breaking Boxing Day win in 1962.

FRIDAY 18TH MARCH 1983

Joe Royle completed his first signing when he brought Tony Henry to Boundary Park from Bolton Wanderers for a fee of £21,000.

TUESDAY 18TH MARCH 2003

Goalkeeper Les Pogliacomi earned his 17th shut-out of the season in a 0-0 draw at Kenilworth Road. The result left Iain Dowie's men in fourth place in the Division Two table.

SATURDAY 18TH MARCH 2006

A convincing 4-1 victory at Bradford City left Athletic in seventh spot and just two points off a League One play-off position. A first-half blitz from Paul Warne, Luke Beckett and Richard Butcher gave the visitors a 3-0 half-time scoreline. Beckett claimed his second goal eight minutes from the end to round off a successful away trip.

SATURDAY 19TH MARCH 1938

A crowd of over 10,000 witnessed this Third Division (North) home game against Carlisle United. A 3-0 victory left Athletic in fifth place in the league and it was achieved with goals from Tommy Butler, John Diamond and an own goal.

SATURDAY 19TH MARCH 1994

A great performance at Villa Park was needed with Athletic battling to stay in the Premiership. An own goal from Steve Redmond gave Villa the lead but a great fightback saw Darren Beckford and Rick Holden score to hand the Latics a surprising victory which left them just one point away from safety.

SATURDAY 19TH MARCH 2005

League One leaders Luton Town came to Boundary Park but Athletic could only muster 5,809 supporters through the turnstiles. The Latics converted a 1-0 deficit into a 2-1 lead with goals from Chris Killen and Luke Beckett but the Hatters snatched a point with an equaliser scored three minutes into time added on. The home crowd went away disappointed with the result but happy with the performance; one that gave hope that relegation could be avoided.

SATURDAY 20TH MARCH 1965

Athletic played at home and lost 3-1 to Walsall. Before the game manager Les McDowall was dismissed as the team lay in 18th position in the Third Division – not as well-placed as expected. He commented, "That's the way it goes in football, but the parting was an amicable one."

SUNDAY 20TH MARCH 1966

Ian Marshall was born in Liverpool and after the sale of Andy Linighan to Norwich in 1988, manager Joe Royle went back to his old stomping ground at Everton to take him on loan. He soon made the deal permanent and paid out £100,000 for his services. Marshall helped Athletic to six wins and three draws in his first ten games and he established himself as a very useful player.

WEDNESDAY 20TH MARCH 1991

Warned about any complacency by manager Joe Royle, Hull City visited Boundary Park for a Second Division game. Royle had said, "We know there are no easy games, and these matches against teams fighting against relegation are probably the toughest of the lot". Andy Ritchie scored a penalty but Hull went on to win 2-1 and inflict the first home defeat of the season on Athletic.

SATURDAY 20TH MARCH 2004

A howling gale at high-flying Bristol City was the first Division Two away game for new manager Brian Talbot. Ernie Cooksey and Paul Murray powered the Latics to a convincing 2-0 win to record the visitors' third game undefeated under Talbot.

TUESDAY 21ST MARCH 1972

Second-placed in the Third Division, AFC Bournemouth visited Oldham in their quest to maintain an automatic promotion place. A 7,000-plus crowd watched an entertaining game which saw the Latics win 3-1. Goals from Jim Bowie, Keith Bebbington and David Shaw were enough to ensure all the points over their lofty counterparts.

WEDNESDAY 21ST MARCH 1990

Athletic paid a club-record fee when they signed Paul Moulden from AFC Bournemouth. The sum of £225,000 was hardly justified as Moulden made a total of 19 starts, with 22 appearances as substitute, and only scored four goals. He was subsequently bought by Birmingham City.

SATURDAY 21ST MARCH 1998

League One leaders Watford came to Boundary Park and looked to be going home with all the points until Mark Allott scored a last minute goal to give the Latics a 2-2 draw. Adrian Littlejohn got the other Latics marker in front of a less than 6,000 crowd.

SATURDAY 22ND MARCH 2003

Wayne Andrews hit two goals to give Athletic a useful 0-2 victory at Northampton Town. The win left the Latics in third spot in Division Two and still on track for an automatic promotion place.

SUNDAY 23RD MARCH 1947

'Little Dave' Ashworth died in Blackpool. He was recognised as Athletic's first manager, having served from 1906-14 and returning to manage the team from 1923-24. Ashworth sported a waxed mustache and it is noted that he had the ends upturned when the Latics won, down when they had lost and one up and one down after a draw. The bowler-hatted, stern-faced manager obviously had a hidden sense of humour. He remarkably took Oldham from the Lancashire Combination to the First Division in a four-year spell during his first period in charge.

SATURDAY 23RD MARCH 1991

A 2-0 defeat at Blackburn Rovers was only the second time in the season that Athletic had lost two consecutive games. It was a very worrying time for the fans with the end of the season nigh, and with a definite Second Division promotion chance up for grabs.

WEDNESDAY 24TH MARCH 1915

Championship-chasing Athletic visited Bradford City for a First Division game. Around 7,000 spectators filled Valley Parade for a fixture which Bradford eventually won 1-0. The result left the Latics just one point behind leaders Manchester City.

SATURDAY 24TH MARCH 1923

Arsenal brought their mid-table First Division team to bottom-of-the-league Oldham Athletic and went away with a 0-0 draw in front of 13,724 fans. The draw left the Latics firmly rooted at the foot of the table.

SATURDAY 24TH MARCH 1928

Mid-table Port Vale were the visitors to Boundary Park for this Second Division clash. Almost 12,000 people witnessed a hat-trick from George Taylor, and a goal from Bert Watson, which earned Athletic a creditable 4-1 victory.

MONDAY 24TH MARCH 2008

Third-placed in League One, Doncaster Rovers were forced to drop valuable points as Oldham earned a useful 1-1 away point. Rovers held the lead at half-time but Jason Jarrett earned the visitors a share of the spoils with a left-foot volley in the 52nd minute. The result was a fair reflection on the balance of play.

TUESDAY 25TH MARCH 1980

Jimmy Frizzell celebrated ten years as manager of Oldham Athletic. The season brought the best points total for the club since they had won promotion. They achieved 43 points and finished in a creditable 11th place in the Second Division table.

SATURDAY 25TH MARCH 2006

A Luke Beckett hat-trick did the damage against Lancashire neighbours Blackpool in a 3-1 win. After scoring two at Bradford, he made his total five goals in a week in the League One game which entertained the 6,480 supporters in attendance.

SUNDAY 26TH MARCH 1978

Goalscorer Albert Pynegar died in Basford, Nottinghamshire. He joined Athletic in July 1925 from Coventry City for a fee of £1,200 and started as centre-forward but moved to inside-right to accommodate Arthur Ormston. The move was a success as Ormston scored a hat-trick against Fulham on his debut followed by five goals just two days later against Stoke City. In 1926/27 and 1927/28 Pynegar was leading scorer with 19 goals. The following season, with only one win from the first ten games, Pynegar was transferred to Port Vale in a deal involving Stewart Littlewood coming to Boundary Park. He played in 138 games and got 55 goals.

WEDNESDAY 26TH MARCH 1980

Ritchie Wellens was born in Moston, Manchester. He made 101 appearances for Athletic and scored 8 goals after he was signed on a free transfer from Blackpool in June 2005. He turned down an offer to stay at Boundary Park and moved to League One rivals Doncaster Rovers in July 2007.

SATURDAY 27th MARCH 1915

A 1-0 win over The Wednesday left Athletic top of the First Division and their opponents in third place, just one point behind. Arthur Gee got the all important goal which clinched the victory.

SATURDAY 27th MARCH 1954

Bottom-of-the-division Athletic gave Leeds United a lesson in finishing with an impressive 4-2 win over their mid-table visitors. Joseph Harris and Frank Scrine got two goals apiece in the Second Division victory.

SATURDAY 27th MARCH 2004

The Latics were embarrassed by bottom-of-the-league Wycombe Wanderers who went away from Boundary Park with a 3-2 win in this Division Two game. Paul Murray and David Eyre got the Latics goals but it was not enough to stop the Chairboys from gaining their first away victory of the season.

WEDNESDAY 28th MARCH 1990

Athletic lost at home to Sheffield United and in the process their 38-game unbeaten home record. It was a bad defeat which meant that the Latics would lose out on a Second Division promotion play-off spot by three points.

SATURDAY 29th MARCH 1913

Athletic made their first-ever appearance in an FA Cup semi-final when they visited Blackburn Rovers' Ewood Park ground to entertain Aston Villa. In a half-full stadium – 22,616 fans – the Latics went down 1-0 to a Stephenson goal in the 32nd minute. Villa keeper Sam Hardy made a good save late on from George Woodger to prevent Athletic from earning a replay. Villa won the cup that season – their fifth victory – when they conquered Sunderland 1-0 in the final at Crystal Palace.

FRIDAY 29th MARCH 1991

It was a Second Division top-two clash between first-placed Oldham and West Ham United, at Boundary Park. An Andy Ritchie penalty in front of 16,932 supporters enabled the Latics to share the spoils with the Hammers after an enthralling and action-packed match. The result left both teams 13 points ahead of third-placed Brighton & Hove Albion.

SATURDAY 29TH MARCH 2008

Ex-Latics player and manager Andy Ritchie brought his Huddersfield Town team to Boundary Park for a League One fixture and Athletic racked up their biggest win of the season. They gave Ritchie's team a footballing lesson with a 4-1 hammering. Jason Jarrett got two goals, Leon Constantine and Chris Taylor completed the scoring. The game was the last in charge for Ritchie as he was fired after the game.

WEDNESDAY 30TH MARCH 1955

Graham Bell was born in Middleton. The son of Tommy Bell, who also played for the Latics, Graham played for Chadderton FC before signing for Oldham as an amateur at the age of 17. He made 187 appearances and scored nine goals before Preston North End manager Nobby Stiles signed him for £80,000.

TUESDAY 31ST MARCH 1970

Athletic gave promotion hopefuls Brentford a shock with a 4-1 hammering at Boundary Park in this Fourth Division game in front of a gate just over 5,000. Goals from Ian Wood, Jim Bowie, Jimmy Fryatt and Keith Bebbington did the damage.

SATURDAY 31ST MARCH 2007

The Latics moved above Yeovil Town after a hard-fought 1-0 victory between two teams both fighting for a play-off spot in League One. The result left both teams with 67 points. Gary McDonald got the only goal of the game in the first half.

OLDHAM ATHLETIC
On This Day

APRIL

SATURDAY 1st APRIL 1922

Athletic lost 2-0 at Anfield to a Liverpool team who topped the First Division. Oldham were left third from the bottom and in a relegation fight.

FRIDAY 1st APRIL 1988

Second-in-the-table Blackburn Rovers were given a healthy whacking by their Lancashire neighbours in a fiercely fought Second Division battle at Boundary Park. Almost 15,000 supporters saw a brace of goals from both Roger Palmer and Andy Ritchie which was enough to see the Latics through.

WEDNESDAY 2nd APRIL 1890

Elliot Pilkington was born in Radcliffe. He made his debut in the match against Notts County on 2nd December 1911, a 2-1 home reverse. He had a chequered career at Oldham with plenty of ups and downs but went on to make 280 appearances while pitching in with 15 goals. Elliot died on 23rd November 1945, in Bury.

MONDAY 2nd APRIL 1956

Although struggling in the Third Division (North), Athletic still managed to hammer Bradford Park Avenue by 5-1. The goals were scored by Tommy Walker, Kenny Chaytor, Don Travis, George Crook and Ron Fawley.

SATURDAY 3rd APRIL 1915

In the 58th minute of the game at Middlesbrough, Billy Cook was sent off by the referee but the bald full-back refused to leave the field of play. The game was abandoned and Cook was suspended for 12 months which probably had a big bearing on Athletic failing to win their first-ever First Division championship.

FRIDAY 3rd APRIL 1925

Goalkeeper, and father of Chris, Fred Ogden was born in Oldham. He was a regular from 1948 to 1951 when a fractured collarbone during the match at Valley Parade cost him his place. Although lightly built, he was very agile. He appeared 167 times in two spells of service. Ogden was put in charge of the juniors and was then made reserve team trainer, a position he held until 1972.

SATURDAY 3rd APRIL 1926

Ken Brierley was born in Ashton-under-Lyne. The inside-left scored his first goal at Anfield in a 3-2 loss but Liverpool came back three years later and signed him for what was then a large sum of £7,000. When Billy Wootton became manager he tried Brierley out on the left wing where he was an instant success with an ability to send over a dangerous cross. He came back for a second spell at Boundary Park in the 1952/53 season and replaced the injured player-manager George Hardwick. He also helped the Latics to win the Third Division (North) championship. He scored 11 goals in 134 games for Oldham. Ken died in Blackpool in 2002.

TUESDAY 4th APRIL 1989

Roger Palmer scored a magnificent diving header to smash Eric Gemmell's all-time scoring record for Athletic which he had held for 35 years. The game was a Second Division fixture against Ipswich Town and the goal was his 110th for the club. The game was won 4-0 and was witnessed by Gemmell himself.

MONDAY 4th APRIL 1994

Table-topping Manchester United visited Boundary Park for a Premiership game which they won 3-2. The result left the Latics just one place above the relegation zone.

TUESDAY 5th APRIL 1955

Kenny Clements was born in Middleton and was signed as a record transfer for Athletic when they paid Manchester City £200,000 in 1979. He struck up a great partnership with Paul Futcher and soon became one of the crowd's favourites. A great player in the air, he went on to appear 182 times in the league for the Latics, scoring two goals.

SATURDAY 5th APRIL 2003

Barnsley came to town to try to put a dent in Athletic's Division Two promotion aspirations. In an exciting game in front of 6,191 supporters, goals from Wayne Andrews and Josh Low were enough to see the home side edge out the Tykes 2-1.

FRIDAY 6TH APRIL 1883

Centre-half Charlie Roberts was born. Athletic paid a record fee of £1,750 in 1913 to entice him away from Manchester United in a move that shocked the footballing world. He helped lead the Latics to fourth place in the First Division – in a season where he was an ever-present – as well as getting the runners up spot the following season. In July 1921 he was appointed manager to succeed Mr Herbert Bamlett, a role that he found very stressful; he could be seen pacing up and down behind the grandstand during the game. He was eventually replaced by David Ashworth in January 1923.

THURSDAY 7TH APRIL 1921

Record scorer Eric Gemmell was born in Prestwich and after a spell as an amateur with Manchester United he turned professional with Manchester City in 1946. Gemmell joined Athletic in 1947 and went on to become one the club's best-ever forwards. He scored an incredible seven goals in an 11-2 hammering of Chester City in 1952 and went on to rack up a total of 120 goals for the club. He was at Boundary Park on the night in 1989 when Roger Palmer broke his record by hitting two goals against Ipswich Town. Eric passed away in February 2008 at the age of 86.

FRIDAY 8TH APRIL 1949

Athletic's most successful manager, Joe Royle, was born in Norris Green, Liverpool. The ex-England international joined Athletic as manager to replace the popular Jimmy Frizzell in June 1982. In his second season in charge the team finished just one point above a relegation place but after some improvement he was offered a new three-year contract in May 1986. In 1986/87 they lost out on promotion in the first-ever play-off games to Leeds United but it was to begin a new era in the fortunes of Oldham Athletic.

FRIDAY 8th APRIL 1949

In 1988-89 the Latics lost just two of their last 20 games and they made it to Wembley for the first time for the League Cup final in 1990 and a year later Joe Royle was named Second Division Manager of the Year as his team swept to the championship to return Athletic to the First Division after a break of 68 years.

SUNDAY 8th APRIL 1990

Maine Road was the venue for this FA Cup semi-final against Manchester United and 44,026 people showed up to see if the remarkable Second Division outfit from Oldham could continue their amazing exploits in their most successful season ever. It was only the second time that Athletic had appeared at this stage but for United it was 'old hat' as it was their 18th appearance.

The Latics scored first through Earl Barrett but Bryan Robson equalised before Neil Webb headed United ahead for the first time. A goal from Ian Marshall took the tie to extra time. Danny Wallace thought he had done enough when he scored but Roger Palmer ghosted in to make it a thrilling 3-3 draw to force a replay. The game was televised in 26 countries and there could not have been many who did not enjoy the enthusiasm and style of both competing teams on a day when sportsmanship and football were the winners.

SATURDAY 9th APRIL 1932

Table-topping Wolverhampton Wanderers demolished Athletic by a score of 7-1 in the Second Division game. Over 20,000 spectators at Molineux roared on the Wolves. Bill Hasson got the lone Oldham goal.

SATURDAY 9th APRIL 1988

Stoke City were hammered 5-1 at Boundary Park in a Second Division match that left Athletic just one point behind their visitors with two games in hand. Roger Palmer hit a hat-trick while Andy Ritchie and Aaron Callaghan added the others.

MONDAY 9TH APRIL 2007

A late goal by Luigi Glombard spoiled the party for Bradford City in what was billed a must-win game for them. The Bantams looked to be holding on for their first home win since December but the late goal left them staring relegation from League One in the face for the first time in 25 years. The 1-1 draw left Athletic in sixth place.

SATURDAY 10TH APRIL 1976

A thumping 5-2 win over Portsmouth finally put paid to worrying doubts if Athletic could maintain their stature in their second season back in the Second Division. They still made hard work of it, though, by taking just one point from their last four matches to finish in 17th place with 38 points.

SATURDAY 10TH APRIL 1994

Athletic met Manchester United at Wembley Stadium in the FA Cup semi-final. The game went to extra time and the Latics took the lead through full-back Neil Pointon with just 13 minutes of the game left. Mark Hughes broke the hearts of Athletic by scoring a last minute volley to deprive the Latics of their first-ever FA Cup Final appearance. Latics fans – to this day – still feel that "that goal" was the one which caused the club's demise and their subsequent drop down to the third level of English football.

THURSDAY 11TH APRIL 1935

Goalkeeper Johnny Bollands was born in Middlesbrough. The former England under-23 and Bolton Wanderers player had two spells with Athletic and made 154 senior league appearances in a distinguished career.

SATURDAY 10TH APRIL 1915

Sheffield United lost 3-0 at Athletic and the win was enough for the Latics to leapfrog Manchester City to become league leaders in Division One with 44 points. The previous game was a 1-0 win over bottom team Manchester United. Oldham finished the season as runners-up to Everton, their highest finish ever.

LATICS CELEBRATE NEIL POINTON'S FA CUP SEMI-FINAL GOAL IN APRIL 1994

WEDNESDAY 11TH APRIL 1990

A significant day in the history of Oldham Athletic as they lost out on their chance to go to Wembley for two finals in one season, and also their chance to appear in an FA Cup final for the first time. Playing Manchester United in an FA Cup semi-final replay at Maine Road, they matched their First Division counterparts and were unlucky not to get through. A television replay confirmed that Nick Henry's seventh minute shot hit the crossbar and bounced down over the line.

Referee Joe Worrall waved play on as he didn't have access to any technology to prove any different. A crowd of 35,005 saw Brian McClair fire United in front only for Andy Ritchie to hammer a left-footer into the roof of the net to put Athletic level. As with so many other contests that season, it would take a period of extra time to settle the result. Local lad Mark Robins scored the winner to put United through but little Oldham had nothing to be ashamed of as they did themselves and the town proud to get so far in an unbelievable season.

TUESDAY 11TH APRIL 2000

Oldham Athletic took on promotion hopefuls Wigan Athletic and came out on top with a 2-1 victory in this Division Two game. The result left the Boundary Park Latics in 11th position, 23 points behind the JJB Stadium Latics in second spot.

SATURDAY 12TH APRIL 2003

A 1-1 draw at Cheltenham Town was hardly the expected result to bolster Athletic's automatic promotion hopes. A goal down after two minutes, the Latics were always chasing the game but David Eyres earned a point with a header in the 31st minute. The result left just four games to go to determine whether Division Two promotion would be gained or if the Latics would have to do it the hard way via the play-offs.

MONDAY 13TH APRIL 1964

Popular goalkeeper Andy Goram was born in Bury. The Scottish international played in 212 games in his six years at the club before moving to Hibernian for £325,000 in 1987. He became the first player to represent their country in the World Cup while playing for Oldham when he appeared in the 1986 finals in Mexico. He was re-signed on emergency short-term loan. Instead of the prodigal son returning as a hero, Cardiff City ran rampant on his return debut winning 7-1, their best-ever win at Boundary Park.

FRIDAY 13TH APRIL 1979

It was Good Friday and Athletic were staring relegation in the face when Blackburn Rovers came to town. With only seven wins in 33 outings, the Latics were two points adrift of Cardiff City who occupied 19th spot in the Second Division. In a game watched by 10,056, Alan Young scored his first Football League hat-trick to help Athletic to a 5-0 mauling of their Lancashire neighbours. An own goal and a Simon Stainrod strike completed the rout. The win was to springboard Oldham to a revival as they lost only one of their last nine league games, finishing in a respectable 14th place.

FRIDAY 13TH APRIL 1979

Fred Worrall died in Warrington. Worrall was an England international who also played for a Football League XI. Athletic stumbled across his services after Bolton Wanderers had been fined £50 for irregularities in his signing from non-league football. Bolton were refused permission to sign him and Athletic jumped in to get him on a free transfer. Recognised as one of the best wingers in the game, he spent three years at Oldham, played 105 league games and scored 20 goals.

SATURDAY 13TH APRIL 1991

New manager of Second Division Newcastle United, Ossie Ardiles, led his team to a 3-2 victory over the visiting Oldham Athletic. Ian Marshall and Rick Holden got the Latics goals in front of a 16,615 crowd.

SATURDAY 14TH APRIL 1945

It was an emotional day at Boundary Park as 857 supporters held a one minute silence in the pouring rain in respect for President Roosevelt who had died the day before. As the Last Post was played a Spitfire overhead dipped in salute. Centre-forward Cottrill put the Latics ahead minutes into the game and they went on to beat Tranmere Rovers 2-1. The previous week Oldham had suffered a 7-1 reverse at Prenton Park.

TUESDAY 15TH APRIL 1947

After a long struggle with the government's ban on midweek soccer, Athletic were granted permission to play a benefit game for Tommy Williamson who had been with Athletic between 1935 and 1947. Around 22,000 people paid a total of £1,149 for the event for Williamson. He was a popular player who had made 157 league appearances for the Latics and scored four goals. He left Oldham to take over as player-manager of Fleetwood.

SATURDAY 16TH APRIL 1949

Almost 18,000 supporters crammed into Boundary Park for the visit of Carlisle United for this Third Division (North) fixture. Eric Gemmell got the only goal of the game in a 1-0 win for the home side.

FRIDAY 16TH APRIL 1965

In an entertaining game against Queens Park Rangers at Boundary Park, the thrilling encounter witnessed Athletic emerge victorious with a 5-3 win. The Latics scorers on the day were Jim Bowie (2), Albert Quixall (pen) and Jimmy Frizzell (2). A crowd of almost 8,000 witnessed the game.

SATURDAY 17TH APRIL 1971

Close promotion rivals Colchester United visited Boundary Park with just four games of the Third Division season left. In front of an ecstatic 10,405 spectators the Latics did a useful job on the Us by hammering them 4-0. Keith Bebbington scored two goals, David Shaw netted and an own goal completed the annihilation and kept the Latics on course.

SATURDAY 17TH APRIL 2004

Division Two leaders Plymouth Argyle came to visit the Latics but goals for the home side from Jermain Johnston, Gareth Owen, David Eyres and Paul Murray gave the home side a comprehensive 4-1 victory. The win hauled Athletic up to 16th spot, just two places above the relegation places but without the three points gained they would have now occupied a drop-zone berth.

SATURDAY 18TH APRIL 1908

A 5-0 hammering of Stockport County left Athletic in second place in the Second Division, just two points behind leaders Bradford City. Henry Hancock, Joe Shadbolt, 'Wilkie' Ward and Frank Newton (2) were the goalscorers.

FRIDAY 18TH APRIL 1930

A crowd of over 24,000 at Bloomfield Road saw Blackpool beat the Latics 3-0 in this top-of-the-table clash. With both teams on 51 points with 37 games played, the result leapfrogged the Seasiders above Oldham to the Second Division summit.

MONDAY 19TH APRIL 1971

The 1970/71 season promotion spots were finely balanced as Athletic visited York City for their 44th Division Four match of the campaign. York were in fourth place, just one point behind Athletic with a game in hand. Bootham Crescent was filled with 14,626 excited spectators, the biggest gate in five years, as the Latics put in their best performance of the season to come away 1-0 victors. The home side were hoping to maintain a 15-month unbeaten record but a Maurice Whittle goal put paid to that plan.

TUESDAY 19TH APRIL 1977

Ian Robins made his 200th appearance for Athletic as they took on Chelsea in a Second Division match that ended in a 0-0 draw at Boundary Park. The Latics team on that day contained no fewer than five players who had made the magical number of 200 appearances. Leading the list was record-breaking Ian Wood with 408, followed by Maurice Whittle (305), Ronnie Blair (232) and David Shaw (207).

SATURDAY 19TH APRIL 2003

A 4-0 thumping of Chesterfield, combined with Crewe Alexandra and Cardiff City losing, set up an exciting end to the season in the race for second spot in Division Two. The Spireites were ripped apart by goals from Wayne Andrews, a brace by Clyde Wijnhard, and a solitary strike from David Eyres in front of almost 7,000 spectators.

MONDAY 19TH APRIL 2004

Former England captain and Athletic player-boss George Hardwick died in Middlesbrough. He took Athletic from 21st position to promotion in 1952-53 and was a popular figure who revitalised a struggling team. He signed from Middlesbrough for £15,000 and appeared 217 times.

SATURDAY 20TH APRIL 1974

Athletic assured themselves of promotion to the Second Division when Huddersfield Town visited Boundary Park. Ronnie Blair opened the scoring with the first two goals then Alan Groves netted with a left-foot effort before a Dolan own goal made it 4-0 at the interval. A penalty from Maurice Whittle and a sixth goal from George McVitie completed the rout in front of 16,466 exultant fans who stormed the pitch at the end of the game to mob their conquering heroes.

SATURDAY 21ST APRIL 1930

A crowd of 45,120 against Blackpool in this Second Division game broke the previous best league gate. The Seasiders won 2-1 and receipts of £2,458 17s 6d were taken on the gate.

SATURDAY 21ST APRIL 1956

George Hardwick resigned as manager after falling attendances, due to poor progress on the field. Athletic would have had to apply for re-election for the first time in their history had it not been for the seven points they gained from the last six games of the season.

MONDAY 21ST APRIL 2003

Wayne Andrews gave Athletic the lead at Wigan Athletic in just 15 seconds. Playing in a must-win game for automatic promotion, the visitors played with conviction but the Latics went downhill and Wigan pulled off a 3-1 success in this Division Two fixture.

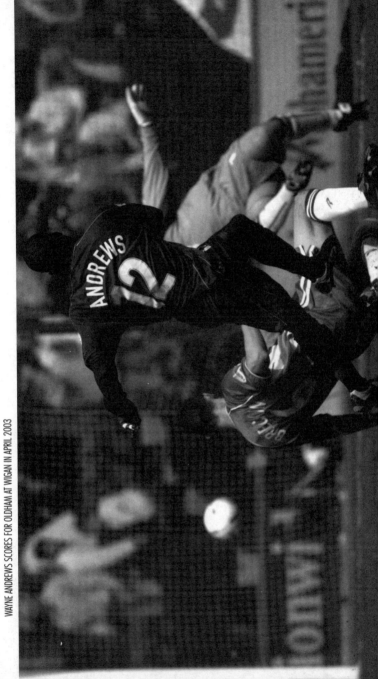

WAYNE ANDREWS SCORES FOR OLDHAM AT WIGAN IN APRIL 2003

FRIDAY 22ND APRIL 2005

Athletic manager Ronnie Moore signed a new two-year contract to keep him at Boundary Park. The Latics were still in 19th place in League One after earning a fine 2-2 away draw at Barnsley with goals by Chris Killen and Luke Beckett.

SATURDAY 23RD APRIL 2005

Torquay United brought their side to Boundary Park for a six-pointer as both sides were struggling at the wrong end of League One. The Gulls pulled off their third consecutive away win as Athletic put in one of their worst performances under Ronnie Moore, who had just signed a new contract the previous day. David Eyres put the home side ahead in the first half but the Devonshire side pulled themselves out of the drop zone with two goals to leave themselves just one point behind the Latics with two games remaining.

SATURDAY 24TH APRIL 1909

Defender Beau Ratcliffe was born in Bolton-on-Dearne, Yorkshire. With New Brighton in financial difficulties Athletic swooped to sign him. A commanding figure anywhere in the back line, Ratcliffe went on to become team captain. He scored once in 162 appearances. His career ended at Oldham with the outbreak of war when all the players' contracts were cancelled after the Football League was suspended. He returned to play for Reading and Watford after the hostilities.

SATURDAY 24TH APRIL 1915

The Latics lost 2-0 at home to Liverpool in the final First Division game of the season and also lost out on their first chance of the league championship. Everton pipped them at the post by one point to leave Athletic to finish as runners-up, their highest-ever league placing.

SATURDAY 24TH APRIL 1971

Chester City lost at Exeter City, and Grimsby Town defeated Colchester United, so a 0-0 draw in front of a miserly 2,239 fans at Workington was enough to get Athletic promoted to the Third Division.

SATURDAY 25TH APRIL 1964

Athletic travelled to Selhurst Park to take on Third Division championship-chasing Crystal Palace in the last game of the season. In an amazing ten minute spell, Bob Ledger scored a hat-trick and Athletic went on to win 3-1. The majority of the almost 28,000 crowd went home disappointed as Palace finished as runners-up on goal difference.

MONDAY 26TH APRIL 1897

Full-back Sammy Wynne was born in Neston. His first two seasons at Athletic were spent in the reserve team but the next three and a half years were spent on first-team duties. He scored nine goals in 145 league games for Athletic and had the distinction of scoring two goals for – and two against – in a match against Manchester United in 1923, a game that the Latics won 3-2! He died in the dressing room at Bury after collapsing on the field in a game against Sheffield United.

TUESDAY 26TH APRIL 1949

An amazing 35,268 supporters turned up to watch the 1-1 draw with Hull City in a season where the Latics averaged a 14,500 gate in the Third Division (North). The club's directors were so pleased with the turn-outs that they offered the manager Billy Wootton a new two-year contract which he gratefully accepted.

SATURDAY 26TH APRIL 2003

With two games remaining the Latics needed just two points to secure a play-off spot. Swindon Town were the visitors and a nervous 6,873 supporters made their way to Boundary Park in trepidation. In an up and down season, the Latics could at least boast that they had never had two consecutive losses. The majority of the fans needn't have worried as the home side comfortably dispatched the opposition. Goals from Josh Low, David Eyres, Will Haining and Carlo Corazzin gave the Blues their second consecutive 4-0 home victory to secure the elusive Division Two play-off spot.

SATURDAY 26TH APRIL 2008

The game against Cheltenham Town was the final League One contest of the season and the last match to be watched by fans in the old Broadway Road stand. The stand was built in the early 1970s with money won in the Ford Sporting League, but it was to be demolished in the summer to make way for a new main stand as part of the Oldham Arena project. The game was won 2-1 with goals from Deane Smalley and Lewis Alessandra and a three-sided stadium was to be found when supporters returned for pre-season friendlies.

SATURDAY 27TH APRIL 1991

Almost 3,000 travelling fans made the long journey to East Anglia to see if Athletic could secure an automatic promotion place to the First Division by winning at Ipswich Town. Just a year after stepping out at Wembley for the first time, Ian Marshall bagged two goals to give the travelling Blue Army the 2-1 result they needed to send them into delirium. The win ensured that First Division football would be played at Boundary Park the following season for the first time in 68 years. Manager Joe Royle said: "I won't say it's an anti-climax, but I thought early on that the top three were the best sides. Eighty points will always get you up. The players are elated, but it isn't as if someone scored the winner in the last ten minutes of the last game. Promotion seems to have been with us for a long time."

SATURDAY 28TH APRIL 1923

A trip to Cardiff coincided with the first-ever Wembley FA Cup final between West Ham United and Bolton Wanderers. The Latics lost 2-0 and it was to be their last First Division away fixture for 68 years as they got relegated for the first time in the club's history at the end of the campaign.

SUNDAY 28TH APRIL 1946

Billy Porter died in the Manchester Royal Infirmary at the early age of 40. He signed for Athletic in May 1926 and made his first team debut in the 3-1 home win against Southampton on 31st January 1928 when two goals from Cliff Stanton and one from Jack King ensured victory and extended Athletic's unbeaten run to 13 league matches. He scored one goal, a penalty, in 284 appearances.

SATURDAY 28th APRIL 1956

Having resigned the previous week, ex-manager George Hardwick played his last game for Athletic. He bowed out in a Third Division (North) 1-1 draw with Wrexham, played at Boundary Park. He said, "There is no ill-feeling, I have enjoyed my spell with Athletic, and have made a lot of good friends in Oldham".

TUESDAY 28th APRIL 1959

In the last game of the season Athletic beat Carlisle United by 2-0 in front of a lowly 3,011 crowd. Athletic finished fourth from the bottom of Division Four with just 36 points in their worst season ever. Another embarrassment was that they would have to apply for re-election to the Football League for the first time. A huge sigh of relief could be heard around Boundary Park in May when the club was eventually re-elected.

FRIDAY 28th APRIL 1967

Earl Barrett was born and went on to be a valuable member of the 1990/91 team that won the Second Division championship. He made 217 appearances for Athletic, scoring nine goals, before he signed for Aston Villa for a fee of £1.7 million. The Latics fans used to serenade him with the cry of, "You'll never beat Earl Barrett". He was an ever-present in the marathon 1989/90 season when he completed 65 senior games.

TUESDAY 28th APRIL 1987

Athletic gained a 2-0 win at Stoke City which guaranteed a promotion play-off spot. They finished third in the Second Division with 75 points, a position that would normally have ensured automatic promotion.

WEDNESDAY 29th APRIL 1953

A 0-0 draw at Bradford City in front of 23,580 fans ensured that Athletic would finish one point ahead of Port Vale to clinch the Third Division (North) championship. In those days only one team was promoted and Vale had a better goal average. Player-manager George Hardwick was chaired from the field at the end of the game by the large contingent of enthusiastic Athletic supporters who had made the cross-Pennine trip. It was Athletic's first championship and they became the first Lancashire team to gain promotion from the Third Division (North) to the Second Division.

THURSDAY 29TH APRIL 1954

One of the first-ever radio commentaries was relayed to patients in both Oldham and Liverpool hospitals when Athletic took on Everton for the last match of the season. Athletic by this time were already relegated and the Toffees won 4-0 to ensure their promotion to Division One.

SUNDAY 29TH APRIL 1990

A fairy tale ended for Athletic as Joe Royle led his team out at Wembley, the first time that the club had ever been there, for the League Cup Final against Nottingham Forest. The match was dubbed 'The Friendly Final' due to the good nature of the opposing fans. Both Forest and Oldham fans were friendly and took pictures of each other on Wembley Way. Nigel Jemson got the only goal of the game but the result did not spoil a great day out for the 30,000 or so Latics supporters who made the trip south, some waiting decades for such an occasion. It was still a memorable end to an unbelievable season.

SATURDAY 30TH APRIL 1910

Athletic entertained Hull City and won 3-0 to secure their first-ever promotion to the First Division, albeit by goal difference and, ironically, over Hull. The Boundary Park gate of 29,083 was a record and many of the ecstatic fans swarmed the field at the end to hail the conquering heroes.

THURSDAY 30TH APRIL 1953

A civic reception was held for Athletic's championship-winning side by the mayor, Councillor HB Whittaker. He complimented them from his parlour, and manager George Hardwick replied, "We as players feel our efforts are appreciated not only by the 'Bob-enders', but by all in the town. I am grateful to the lads of both the first and second teams, and I am also grateful to the directors for tolerating me in the boardroom. We do not always see eye to eye but I usually get my way!"

TUESDAY 30TH APRIL 1974

Needing just one point to win the Third Division championship, Athletic entertained Charlton Athletic in front of 18,528 expectant fans. The Latics, however, fluffed the chance as they went down 2-0.

OLDHAM ATHLETIC
On This Day

MAY

SATURDAY 1st MAY 1926

Athletic enjoyed their biggest league win since they joined the league in 1907 thrashing Nottingham Forest 8-3 in a game at Boundary Park. The win ensured that the Latics would finish in seventh position in the Second Division.

SATURDAY 1st MAY 2004

John Eyre scored both goals in a 2-0 win over Chesterfield at Boundary Park. Over 8,000 spectators watched the game and by the end of the day the Spireites were sitting third from the bottom of the Division Two table.

SATURDAY 2nd MAY 1925

Crystal Palace (34 points) was the venue of the final Second Division game of the season where Athletic needed a draw to retain their Second Division status. Jack Keedwell scored the only goal of the match to ensure that Athletic (35 points) were saved from relegation. Unfortunately for Palace they, along with Coventry City, were one of the teams to receive a drop in status.

WEDNESDAY 2nd MAY 1962

Centre-forward Micky Quinn was born in Liverpool. Quinn played in 86 league games for the Latics in the 1980s and was a crowd pleaser with his quick turns and sharp eye for goal. Manager Joe Royle signed him from Stockport County for a fee of £52,000. He scored 37 goals before being transferred to Portsmouth in 1984 for £150,000.

FRIDAY 3rd MAY 1974

The final match of the season was played at Plymouth Argyle's Home Park ground. With the Latics needing a draw to win the Third Division championship, a large contingent of travelling supporters made the long journey to watch the game. Athletic did not disappoint as they held on for a 0-0 result. Maurice Whittle became a hero that night for kicking a goal-bound effort off the line. Athletic had done it and returned to the Second Division after a break of 20 years.

SATURDAY 3RD MAY 2003

With a Division Two play-off spot already secured the Latics made the short trip to Huddersfield Town for the final league game of the season. The Terriers were already relegated and former Athletic boss Mick Wadsworth had gone, so Huddersfield were playing for pride while the Latics wanted a win to finish in third place. Town took the lead only for Tony Carrs to level with a low skimming drive. The 1-1 draw left Athletic in fifth spot with the prospect of two games against Queens Park Rangers standing in their way to the final of the play-offs.

SATURDAY 4TH MAY 1935

West Ham went away from Boundary Park with a 2-0 win leaving the Latics with their highest goals against total since they entered the league almost 30 years previously. They had a dreadful campaign and conceded 95 goals, as well as being the only team in the four divisions not to win an away game all season. They managed just three draws on their travels and finished next to the bottom of the Second Division with just 26 points, one better than bottom club Notts County.

TUESDAY 4TH MAY 1982

Charlton Athletic visited Boundary Park for a game in which Andy Goram made his debut. With only 2,904 supporters – the worst attendance since Athletic were promoted to the Second Division – bothering to show up, the Latics won 1-0 with Ged Keegan getting the only goal.

SATURDAY 5TH MAY 1923

Athletic beat Cardiff City by 3-1 but it was too little too late and the Latics finished bottom of the First Division and were relegated. Harry Horrocks scored the third goal and few people would have thought that it would be another 68 years until Athletic fans saw another First Division strike. Earl Barrett scored the next historical goal at Liverpool in the first game of the 1991/92 season.

SATURDAY 5TH MAY 2007

The 1-0 win over Chesterfield, witnessed by 8,148 fans, was enough to ensure that the Latics would be in the League One play-off finals for the first time since 2003. They ended the season in sixth position and three points ahead of Swansea City who got hammered at home 6-3 by Blackpool, the team that Athletic were to meet in the play-offs. Chris Porter got the only goal, his 23rd of the season.

SATURDAY 6TH MAY 1922

A 3-1 win over Aston Villa was just the tonic for struggling Athletic in this First Division game at Boundary Park. Reuben Butler, William Wood and Bert Watson got the goals in front of a 12,527 gate. The loss still left Villa in a handily-placed fifth spot.

SATURDAY 6TH MAY 2000

Luton Town entertained Athletic for this final match of the season in the Second Division. It looked like the Hatters were on course for a victory but Matthew Tipton scored a goal in the last minute to ensure a share of the spoils for the Latics. The result left the Bedfordshire outfit one place, and one point, above their guests in 13th position.

SATURDAY 7TH MAY 1966

Bill Taylor died in Southwell. Taylor made 110 league appearances and scored one goal in a career at Boundary Park that lasted from 1920 to 1925. He gave great service to the Latics and played in all three half-back positions.

TUESDAY 7TH MAY 1974

A civic reception was held at Oldham Town Hall to celebrate Athletic's championship-winning side. Mr Sam Bolton, vice-chairman of the Football League, was there to present the Third Division championship trophy. Andy Lochhead was captain of the team and Colin Garwood finished the season as leading marksman. The average home gate for the season was 10,356 and Athletic were back in the Second Division after too long a break.

TUESDAY 7TH MAY 1991

Athletic beat Second Division play-off hopefuls Middlesbrough by 2-0 at Boundary Park. The ground was in an eerie state with work having already commenced on the Chaddy End. The roof was partially removed in preparation for the changeover to a 3,200 all-seater stand. With 14,213 fans roaring them on, Ian Marshall and Rick Holden got the goals to see off the visitors. Boro did finish in the last play-off spot by goal difference.

SATURDAY 7TH MAY 1994

There was a carnival atmosphere at Carrow Road. Over 1,500 Latics fans made the trip to Norfolk to see if their team could preserve their Premiership status with a victory over Norwich City. Unfortunately, the 1-1 draw sealed the visitors' fate and Athletic were down, but not buried. The visiting fans outsung the Canaries fans throughout the game, and afterward a hardy bunch stayed singing in the rain to salute their heroes for giving them three magnificent years in the top flight. Not there to mourn, the fans were there to celebrate on an emotionally-charged afternoon.

SATURDAY 7TH MAY 2005

A total of 9,371 fans showed up for the visit of Bradford City in a match that could have seen Athletic enter into the record books as being the first-ever Premiership team to crash to the bottom of the league pyramid. However, a 2-1 win ensured that they would remain in League One. Goals by Chris Killen and Luke Beckett were enough as Milton Keynes' win over Torquay United was sufficient to send the Gulls down to the basement league, albeit by goal difference.

SATURDAY 8TH MAY 1999

Reading visited Boundary Park with Athletic looking for a victory to secure their Second Division status. They managed a 2-0 win on the day. Mark Innes hit the target but the goal from Paul Rickers was probably one of his most important ever. The Latics avoided relegation by one point.

THURSDAY 9TH MAY 1963

Richard Jobson was born in Holderness, Yorkshire. Manager Joe Royle brought him to Boundary Park in the promotion-winning season of 1990/91 for a record sum of £460,000. He was able to make the signing after the dispensing of the services of Mike Milligan, Denis Irwin and Andy Rhodes. In the third match of the Latics' first season in the First Division, Jobson fractured his cheekbone against Norwich City. He moved to Leeds United for £1m but injuries restricted his appearances and he transferred to Manchester City to again join up with Joe Royle. He completed 225 games, scoring 11 goals, for the Latics over a period of five years.

FRIDAY 9TH MAY 1975

Midfielder Paul Rickers, who joined Oldham Athletic as a 14-year-old, was born in Pontefract. He made his league debut for the Latics in a 0-0 draw at home to Stoke City on 22nd October 1994. Rickers refused manager Iain Dowie's contract offer of extending his stay at Boundary Park in 2002 and instead joined Northampton Town on a two-year deal after scoring 22 goals in 293 appearances. A broken leg restricted his chances at the Cobblers so he moved to Leigh RMI on loan but his contract was later cancelled and he was sadly unable to resurrect his career.

SATURDAY 9TH MAY 1987

Mike Cecere took home the match ball when Blackburn Rovers came to visit Boundary Park for the final Second Division game of the season. Cecere scored all three goals in a convincing 3-0 win over their Lancashire rivals.

TUESDAY 10TH MAY 1966

A Third Division relegation battle between Athletic and York City resulted in a 3-0 win for the Latics. Ian Towers, Jimmy Frizzell and Billy Dearden got the goals. Athletic escaped relegation by one point but York dropped to the Fourth Division.

TUESDAY 10TH MAY 1994

Goalkeeper Paul Gerrard was named in the England under-21 squad for the Toulon tournament in France. Also on this day, Roger Palmer was handed a free transfer after 13 and a half years at the club, after netting an amazing 159 times. He admitted, "It will be strange not coming in after so many years. It makes you feel as though you are getting divorced". Jimmy Frizzell, who signed Palmer in 1980 added, "It has given me great pleasure to see Roger do so well".

SATURDAY 10TH MAY 2003

Over 12,000 crammed in to Boundary Park to witness the first Division Two play-off game against Queens Park Rangers. The Rangers were in aggressive form but their petulance earned them six yellow cards and a sending off. Athletic took the lead in the 27th minute from a David Eyres free-kick that took a deflection. It was a mistake from the home keeper that gave QPR a lifeline. Miskelly flapped around and left a gaping hole for Langley to score from a cross. The final score was 1-1 which left everything to play for in the next encounter in London.

SATURDAY 11TH MAY 1963

The 1962/63 season ended with Athletic as runners-up and promoted to the Third Division. However, behind the scenes a row had been brewing and as a result the board asked for the resignation of manager Jack Rowley before midnight. Les McDowell took over the reins.

SATURDAY 11TH MAY 1968

The Latics ended a disastrous season with a 5-3 home reverse to Bristol Rovers in front of a paltry gate of just over 2,000. They finished in 17th place in the Third Division with an average attendance of around 6,000 which was an all-time low. Things were not going to plan for chairman Ken Bates and falling numbers contributed to the ceased production of the *Boundary Bulletin*, voted the second best programme in the Football League.

SATURDAY 11TH MAY 1985

The 5-2 hammering of Carlisle United was witnessed by an embarrassing gate of just 2,470 in a Second Division fixture.

SATURDAY 11TH MAY 1991

In one of the most remarkable and memorable games ever staged at Boundary Park, Sheffield Wednesday came to spoil the party for championship-seeking Athletic. It was the last day of the season and West Ham United were in top spot in the Second Division, Athletic were second and Wednesday occupied third spot.

To make it even more interesting the Hammers were entertaining fourth-placed Notts County. West Ham lost 2-1 at home to the Meadow Lane outfit but as news filtered through to them that Athletic were losing 2-0 at home the celebrations began at Upton Park.

Athletic remarkably pulled back the score to 2-2 in regulation time and even a draw would be enough to give the Londoners the trophy. With all other games ended, referee Vic Callow allowed more time to compensate for the Yorkshire club's time-wasting antics. After 92 minutes of pulsating football, future Latics boss John Sheridan brought down Andy Barlow for a penalty to the home side. The penalty became the last kick, of the last game, on the last day of the season! It just couldn't have been scripted.

Neil Redfearn stepped up to take the kick but then the referee booked a Sheffield player. It all added to the tension. Cool as a cucumber, Redfearn strode up to plant the penalty – his most important goal ever – home to send Boundary Park into a frenzy. Fans invaded the pitch to celebrate and in true World Cup-type commentary they thought it was all over: well, it was now!

The championship trophy arrived by courier at Boundary Park with West Ham's name engraved on it, much to the embarrassment of Football League officials!

SATURDAY 12TH MAY 1945

Manager Frank Womack gave a debut to 17-year-old centre-half JB Smith from Houghton United. The match was against Liverpool and the youngster had a terrible time as the opponents rattled seven past the frail Latics defence. The temperature was in the 90s as street parties, bunting, bonfires and dancing went on in the streets of Oldham. Well, it was VE Day after all!

SUNDAY 12TH MAY 1991

An open-top bus took the Oldham team and officials from the ground to the Civic Centre for a celebration and official reception to commemorate Athletic's feat of gaining promotion back to the First Division. Around 15,000 Latics fans cheered the team on as they gathered on the Civic Centre balcony. Councillor Jacobs gave a simple message when he said, "Well done Joe, champion, just champion."

SUNDAY 13TH MAY 2007

Athletic entertained Blackpool in the first leg of the League One play-offs. Andy Liddell got the only Latics goal in a 2-1 loss which gave the Seasiders the advantage.

SATURDAY 14TH MAY 1983

The last Second Division match of the season – Joe Royle's first in charge – was a trip to Cambridge United. The Us had put together a 12-match run without a goal being conceded but Athletic put paid to that. Inspired by 20-year-old Darren McDonough the visitors scored four goals in an eight minute spell in the second half, two of them by McDonough, the last being a spectacular header from a John Ryan cross. Athletic won 4-1.

THURSDAY 14TH MAY 1987

The first ever Second Division play-offs took place and Athletic crossed the Pennines to take on Leeds United. In front of 29,472, Athletic were on course for a commendable 0-0 draw but in the final minute, substitute Keith Edwards scored a vital goal to give Leeds the edge for the second leg which was to take place in three days time.

TUESDAY 14TH MAY 1991

Athletic's plastic pitch was torn up. The club were forced to remove it when they got promoted to the First Division. The cost of replacement was £200,000 and it also lost Athletic an annual income from the community of around £45,000.

WEDNESDAY 14TH MAY 2003

Over 17,000 were present at Loftus Road. After a 1-1 draw in Oldham a place in the Division Two play-off final was at stake with this second leg tie against QPR. With around 2,500 Latics fans making the trip to the game and approximately 4,000 watching a beam-back at Boundary Park, it would be a tense match.

It was an end-to-end game with the prospect of one flash of brilliance or one mistake being possibly the difference between the teams. Unfortunately for the Oldham supporters, it was the latter. In the 82nd minute a poor clearance from goalkeeper Les Pogliacomi allowed Rangers to win the match 1-0 and leave the Latics pondering a season that promised so much.

SATURDAY 15TH MAY 1982

Athletic beat the Orient on their home turf by 3-0 in the final game of the season. A Rodger Wylde penalty and goals from Roger Palmer and John Bowden secured the win. The Latics ended the season in 11th place in the Second Division and increased their average home gate from 6,502 to 7,027.

THURSDAY 16TH MAY 1935

Henry Spink was transferred to Rossendale United. Spink was a speedy winger who had made himself a regular first teamer but was placed on the transfer list along with ten others after Athletic faced the prospect of their first-ever season in the Third Division. Spink scored just one goal in 20 league appearances for the Latics.

SATURDAY 17TH MAY 1947

Bill Blackshaw got the only goal of the game as Athletic beat Third Division (North) promotion hopefuls Chester City at Boundary Park in front of 7,378 fans.

SUNDAY 17TH MAY 1987

Leeds United visited Boundary Park for the second leg of the Second Division promotion play-off games, the first year of such fixtures. Leeds were a goal up from the first match but Gary Williams soon put the teams level. Ex-Leeds players Andy Linighan, Tommy Wright and Denis Irwin all played against their old club while future Latics star Andy Ritchie played for Leeds.

Mike Cecere headed what looked like the winner just minutes from the end, but Leeds silenced the home fans when Edwards got his second last-minute goal in two games. The 2-1 final scoreline for the Latics – watched by 19,216 supporters – meant that Leeds went through on the away goals rule. It was a bitter pill for the Boundary Park faithful to swallow, some of whom were openly weeping at the end of the game.

SATURDAY 18TH MAY 1966

The Latics were struggling in the Third Division when they entertained Brighton & Hove Albion with over 10,000 in attendance. Big Jim Bowie scored the only goal of the game to hoist Athletic out of the relegation zone. This is the only recorded game for Athletic on this day.

SATURDAY 19TH MAY 2007

The second leg of the League One play-offs was played at Bloomfield Road with Blackpool leading 2-1 from the first leg. The Seasiders cruised into the Wembley final with a 3-1 win. Matty Wolfenden scored the consolation goal for an under-par Athletic side. Blackpool went on to win the final and returned to level two of the Football League after a break of 28 years.

WEDNESDAY 20TH MAY 1908

Irish international inside-forward William Andrews was signed from Glentoran. Andrews had hit 36 goals in the previous season for Glentoran but he found the task more difficult in England. In his nine league appearances for Athletic he scored three goals but later went on to distinguish himself with Grimsby Town.

WEDNESDAY 21st MAY 1947

A 1-0 loss at York City was all that the struggling Latics could muster at Bootham Crescent in this Third Division (North) campaign. The result left Athletic one point away from York but they did have three games in hand.

WEDNESDAY 21st MAY 1966

A very successful 3-1 win over Oxford United in a Third Division match was well received by the near 8,500 crowd at Oldham. Ian Towers, Jimmy Frizzell and Billy Dearden got the Latics goals.

WEDNESDAY 21st MAY 1986

Denis Irwin was signed by manager Joe Royle on a free transfer from Leeds United. Irwin was to later make a big move to Old Trafford and establish himself as one of the finest full-backs in the country.

MONDAY 22nd MAY 1933

Arthur Bailey joined Athletic for the first of two spells when he signed from Manchester North End. A joiner by trade, he made a total of 53 league appearances and scored 12 goals. He joined the Latics for his second spell after a stint at Stalybridge Celtic just before World War II and became a regular player in wartime football.

TUESDAY 23rd MAY 1967

Eric Magee signed for the Latics from Glenavon for a fee of £4,200. Eric was one of Jimmy McIlroy's group of young Irish signings. The inside-forward made his first-team debut against Peterborough United on 26th August in the same year, although he first played for the Blues on their tour of Rhodesia and Malawi. He made a total of 45 league appearances and scored nine goals.

SATURDAY 24th MAY 1947

The 1-0 win at Hull City was a useful couple of points for Athletic. Almost 15,000 people squeezed into Boothferry Park to see Bill Blackshaw score the only goal of the Third Division (North) game to give the visitors the points. This match is the only recorded game for Athletic on this day.

WEDNESDAY 25TH MAY 1966

Only one Oldham game has been recorded on this day. Athletic lost 2-0 at home to Queens Park Rangers, a result which saw the Latics finish in 20th place in the Third Division.

THURSDAY 26TH MAY 1932

Ian Greaves was born. Although the full-back only made 22 league appearances for the club, he left a big impression. The ex-Manchester United player joined Athletic from Lincoln City for a fee of £2,000 and he went on to manage successfully, including two Second Division titles with both Huddersfield Town (1969/70) and Bolton Wanderers (1977/78).

THURSDAY 27TH MAY 1965

Gordon Hurst was appointed to the Boundary Park hot-seat. In 1964 he was appointed as part-time coach of Athletic reserves after Henry Cockburn left to join Huddersfield Town. His senior side struggled to only three wins in 22 league matches before he was replaced by Jimmy McIlroy in January 1966. He continued as assistant manager until he left in 1967 to join Rochdale as trainer/coach.

SATURDAY 28TH MAY 1960

Athletic were waiting for the results of their second consecutive re-election to the league, having finished the season second from the bottom of Division Four with just 28 points. The annual meeting of the Football League in London resulted in 36 votes for Oldham, the top votes, who were re-elected to Division Four. News was not as good for Gateshead who were voted out and replaced by Peterborough United.

FRIDAY 29TH MAY 1964

Gritty Alan Lawson was signed from Glasgow Celtic. One of the toughest-tackling centre-halves ever to be seen at Boundary Park, Lawson was the first-ever substitute used by Athletic. He replaced Albert Jackson in the home game against Peterborough United on 28th August 1965. Lawson also scored his only goal, in the same fixture, for Athletic in a six-year stay and 138 league appearances.

THURSDAY 30TH MAY 1957

Edmund Shimwell joined Athletic from Blackpool. He had served a distinguished career at the Seasiders where he made 283 appearances. He left them after a dispute over him taking licensed premises. He was a hard-tackling full-back who liked to overlap and he became the first full-back to score a goal in a Wembley final when he notched for the Seasiders in their 1948 FA Cup Final 4-2 defeat to Manchester United. He only made seven starts for Athletic before moving to Burton Albion.

SATURDAY 31ST MAY 1919

Having previously beaten Manchester City 1-0 at home in the Lancashire Cup semi-final replay with a goal from Arthur Gee, Athletic took on Liverpool in the final. The game was played in front of a '22,000' gate at Old Trafford. Liverpool ran out 3-0 winners to lift the cup for the first time in their history. The gate receipts received for the match were £1,305 10s 0d.

OLDHAM ATHLETIC
On This Day

JUNE

WEDNESDAY 1st JUNE 1955

Goalkeeper Jack Hacking died in Accrington. He was a steady professional who played 234 games for the club. He was also selected to play as an England international. At 47, Hacking became the oldest player to appear in a league game in the season 1943-44 when he deputised for his injured son.

THURSDAY 1st JUNE 2006

Manager Ronnie Moore and his assistant John Breckin were sacked and immediately replaced by reserve team coach John Sheridan. Fans pressured for his dismissal after the perceived poor quality of football (or hoof-ball as they described it) on display at the club, and they vowed, in numbers, not to renew their season tickets unless Moore went. Managing Director Simon Corney listened.

FRIDAY 2nd JUNE 1922

Ted Taylor was transferred to Huddersfield Town for a fee of £1,950. He was understudy goalkeeper at Boundary Park to Howard Mathews and played 86 league games for the Latics. He went on to establish himself as the England number one keeper.

WEDNESDAY 2nd JUNE 1954

Outside-left Dennis King signed for Athletic from Spennymoor United for a fee of £350. Athletic had signed four players from this area in the same summer but King was understudy to the reliable Tommy Walker and found it difficult to establish himself in the team. He was a versatile player and scored seven goals in 22 league games before being transferred to Chorley.

FRIDAY 3rd JUNE 1938

Centre-half Alan Williams was born in Bristol. He was fearless and resolute and will be remembered as Athletic's best centre-half of the 1960s. He was an ever-present in the promotion year of 1962/63 and was made team captain. Williams made over 550 league appearances in his 18 years in the game and was a great servant to all his clubs. He scored nine goals in 172 league outings for Athletic.

MONDAY 3RD JUNE 1940

John Colquhoun was born in Stirling and signed for Athletic from Stirling Albion in 1961 for a fee of £6,000. Colquhoun was an ever-present member of Jack Rowley's promotion-winning side of 1962/63. A versatile player, Colquhoun played in every forward position for Athletic and achieved 255 appearances while rattling in 51 goals in his two spells with the club.

THURSDAY 4TH JUNE 1964

Hard-tackling Alan Lawson was signed from Glasgow Celtic. Lawson stayed at Boundary Park for six years and soon became a fans' favourite with his no-nonsense approach to defending. He played in 138 league games for Athletic and scored just one goal, which came against Peterborough United in 1965.

TUESDAY 4TH JUNE 1974

Associate schoolboy Steve Edwards became an apprentice and went on to sign professional forms in 1976. Edwards stayed at Boundary Park between the years of 1974-83 and was successfully converted from midfield to full-back. He was a cool and collected performer who played a total of 80 senior league games for the Latics.

SUNDAY 5TH JUNE 1938

Tommy Davies was snapped up from a French club for the meagre sum of £250 – and what a bargain it turned out to be. His first three months were spent by serving a suspension, imposed for breaking his previous contract. He scored 35 goals in the 1936/37 season, which is still a club record. Davies also marked his international debut for the Irish Free State by scoring two goals against Germany in the same season.

MONDAY 5TH JUNE 1978

Defender/midfielder John Ryan signed as an apprentice at Boundary Park, turning professional in 1980. He made a century of league appearances for the Latics and scored eight goals. A serious double fracture of his left leg, sustained in a friendly game at Tranmere Rovers in 1986, resulted in only one further appearance the following campaign before retiring.

FRIDAY 5TH JUNE 1987

Ian Ormondroyd, more commonly referred to as 'The Stick', completed his loan spell at Athletic. He signed in bizarre fashion from Bradford City just minutes before the transfer deadline after Ron Futcher made the move to the Bantams with a £40,000 fee. Part of the deal included the loan spell until the end of the season. The 6ft 4ins striker was surprisingly ineffective in the air as he scored just one goal in ten league appearances for the Blues. Before representing the Latics, the beanpole forward played for Aston Villa, Derby County, Leicester City and Hull City, to varying levels of success. The Bradford-born ex-player is, at 2008, Football in the Community Officer at his hometown club.

SATURDAY 6TH JUNE 1925

Half-back Ted Goodier signed for the club. He had to wait for his chance to establish himself in the team and his chance came when Jimmy Naylor was transferred to Huddersfield Town. Goodier played 115 league games for the Latics and scored two goals. He later went on to manage the club from 1956-58.

WEDNESDAY 7TH JUNE 1911

Arthur Gee was one of the youngest players ever to sign professional forms for the Latics. The inside-forward was only 5ft 6ins tall but he was a good finisher and a very determined competitor. He managed to score 42 goals in 112 league appearances for the club before moving to Stalybridge Celtic for their first ever season in the Third Division (North).

WEDNESDAY 7TH JUNE 1972

Midfielder Graham Bell signed amateur forms at Boundary Park and went on to become a professional in December 1973. The son of former Latics star Tommy Bell, Graham was a competitive midfield general who played big in spite of his lightly-built frame. He played 170 senior league games and scored nine goals before a big money move to Preston North End in 1979.

SATURDAY 8TH JUNE 1963

Gary Williams, son of former Athletic captain Alan, was born in Bristol. Manager Joe Royle brought him from Bristol Rovers and he established himself as a very competent midfielder. He was an unused substitute in the 1990 League Cup final.

FRIDAY 9TH JUNE 1905

Stalwart Jimmy Hodson signed for Athletic for a fee of £15. He remained at Boundary Park for around ten years and played at levels ranging from the Lancashire Combination up to being First Division runners-up. He scored one goal in his 252 league appearances and was awarded a benefit game with a £250 guarantee for his service.

SATURDAY 9TH JUNE 1956

A fee of £200 was enough to bring goalkeeper David Teece to Boundary Park from Hull City. He had an uncertain start and lost his place to Derek Williams but his final two seasons saw him as first choice keeper. The 6ft stopper made 91 league appearances.

FRIDAY 10TH JUNE 1938

Ernie Wright joined Athletic from Chesterfield. The inside-forward could create space in midfield and played nearly every game in his year at Oldham. Even though he had featured for three league clubs previously he had made just six league starts.

SATURDAY 10TH JUNE 1961

Centre-half Alan Williams was signed from Bristol City for a fee of £1,000 – and what a bargain he turned out to be. He quickly established himself as a favourite of the fans and was an ever-present, captaining the team in the 1962/63 promotion season. He also scored nine league goals, which was a good return from a centre-back.

THURSDAY 11TH JUNE 1953

Ray Clemence's Liverpool goalkeeping understudy, Peter McDonnell, was born in Kendal. McDonnell was very competent and was an ever-present in his first season at Boundary Park. He played 137 times in the league during his four years at Oldham before moving to Barrow, eventually becoming their player-manager.

SUNDAY 12TH JUNE 1938

Stuart Richardson was born in Leeds. He was a member of the team that had the ignominious task of applying for re-election for the second successive year after the 1959/60 season. He made 22 league appearances as a half-back and had to fight the likes of Brian Jarvis and Bill Spurdle for a first team starting position.

SATURDAY 13TH JUNE 1953

Athletic's representatives went to London for the Football League AGM where they were presented with their Third Division (North) championship shield and their winners' medals. They were the only team from Lancashire to gain promotion to the Second Division.

TUESDAY 14TH JUNE 1932

Dashing left winger Colin Whitaker was born in Leeds. He scored 29 goals in 72 league appearances for the Latics and was a true 'wizard of the wing' who scored over one hundred goals, including an amazing eight hat-tricks. A wonderful trapper of the ball, Colin played for Sheffield Wednesday, Shrewsbury Town, Queens Park Rangers and Rochdale, before moving to Oldham. After leaving the Latics he played at Barrow and then became player-manager at Stalybridge Celtic. Colin also played Minor Counties cricket for Shropshire.

MONDAY 14TH JUNE 1982

Jimmy Frizzell was fired from his managerial role after 22 years as a player and manager. The news rocked the football world as the popular Frizzell was the longest-serving manager in the Football League at the time. An official statement declared: "The board has decided to terminate the manager's employment. The two years remaining on his contract will be honoured along with his testimonial arrangements. There is no particular reason for our decision, but we do feel that the club needs a new challenge, and people coming through the turnstiles. We are hoping for a new impetus throughout the club." The responding comment from Mr Frizzell was a diplomatic, "No comment!"

TUESDAY 14TH JUNE 2005

Outside-right Tommy Walker died in Middleton. Signed from Newcastle United, his first appearance added 2,000 extra fans to the Boundary Park gate on 6th February 1954 when he made his debut against Doncaster Rovers in a Third Division (North) game. Bobby McIlvenny and Frank Scrine got the Latics goals in a 2-2 draw. He left the Latics in February 1957 to join Chesterfield for £1,250 but he never settled and returned to Oldham in July of the same year. He scored 23 goals in 164 appearances.

THURSDAY 15TH JUNE 1978

The footballing world was shocked when Alan Groves died on this day, just before his 30th birthday. The ever popular 'Grovesey' was one of the rare breed of entertaining crowd pleasers with his antics on the field. His dazzling footwork was a pleasure to watch and he used to constantly talk to the supporters. Blackpool, his team when he died, came to Boundary Park on 29th July 1978 for a benefit game which was watched by 4,396 loyal, heartbroken fans. Renowned for the 'love beads' around his neck, Groves scored 13 times for Oldham and appeared in 153 games.

TUESDAY 15TH JUNE 1982

The news of long-serving manager Jimmy Frizzell's recent firing came as a shock to the town and protests poured into Boundary Park. Frizzell was a popular figure and fans did not like the prospect of facing the future without him. Calls for a boardroom takeover were vehement.

FRIDAY 16TH JUNE 1967

Athletic flew out from London to Salisbury to begin a tour of Rhodesia and Malawi where they played nine games against the local teams. In Malawi, the National Football Association hosted trial games to select a national team to play Athletic as part of the celebration of the first anniversary of the establishment of Malawi, which was formerly the Central African British Colony of Nyasaland.

MONDAY 17TH JUNE 1963

Ex-Manchester City boss Les McDowall became the new manager at Boundary Park. He said, "It's a great club, and it's riding on the crest of a wave. Consequently, as far as I'm concerned, it will be status quo to start with. You don't start making rash changes when things are going well". The club had just been promoted and the success continued as Athletic led the Third Division but injuries and lack of form kicked in. The Latics finished in ninth place at the end of the season.

MONDAY 18TH JUNE 1962

Lanky centre-back Andy Linighan was born in Hartlepool. At 6ft 2½ins, he was remarkably mobile and occasionally liked to go forward to use his height in attack, a tactic which brought him six goals. Signed from Leeds United for £55,000, his two years and 87 league appearances brought the club a good return when he was sold to Norwich City for £350,000, then a record fee received.

SUNDAY 18TH JUNE 1967

Athletic kicked off their Rhodesia and Malawi tour with a 6-0 win over St. Pauls (Rhodesia National Champions) in Salisbury. Ian Towers got a hat-trick and Keith Bebbington, Eric Magee and Ken Knighton added the other goals.

TUESDAY 19TH JUNE 1951

Outside-left Bill Jessop was transferred to Wrexham in part exchange for Dennis Grainger. He had been signed from Preston North End some three years earlier for a fee of £1,250 and had scored 16 goals in 94 league games for the Latics.

SATURDAY 19TH JUNE 1954

The 'Durham wonderboy' Kenny Chaytor signed as an amateur for Athletic, becoming professional in November of the same year. At 16-years-old, he played for the Latics although he was not old enough to become a professional. He had a good few years at Boundary Park before he drifted into non-league football with Witton Albion at the tender age of 22.

THURSDAY 19TH JUNE 2003

Athletic failed to pay their Inland Revenue monthly bills which could result in the Revenue serving a winding-up order. The club shop had to close its doors and their bank account was frozen. It was so grave that if the players' wages were not paid by 27th June, they could give notice and walk away from the club. Administration was not an option for the Latics, as in the case of a lot of clubs, as they had already disposed of their ground a number of years ago to service previous debts. They were left with no assets whatsoever to convince a judge to grant an administration order.

SUNDAY 20TH JUNE 1965

Neil Redfearn was born in Dewsbury. He will be remembered for eternity at Oldham after scoring probably the most important winning goal ever witnessed at Boundary Park. It came on the last day of the season against Sheffield Wednesday in the 1990/91 season. His penalty ensured that Athletic pipped West Ham to the Second Division championship by one point. The Latics were back in the First Division after a break of 68 years.

WEDNESDAY 21ST JUNE 1967

Athletic suffered their only defeat on the tour of Rhodesia when they went down 3-2 to Rio Tinto in Que Que. The scorers for the Latics were Reg Blore and Bill Asprey (pen) in a game that was played before a crowd of 4,777.

SATURDAY 22ND JUNE 1957

Half-back Bill Spurdle started his second spell at Athletic, his first being as an amateur and a professional in wartime football. Spurdle made 200 league appearances for the Latics and was a 'Chaddy End' favourite. He added 24 league goals to his credentials and was the first Channel Islander to appear in an FA Cup final when he played for Manchester City against Newcastle United in 1955.

THURSDAY 22ND JUNE 1961

Burnley transferred the captain of their reserve side, Jim Scott, to Athletic. Scott gave good service to the Latics and was always cool under pressure. Originally a left-half, he was also comfortable on the right or at full-back. He made 76 league appearances in his time at Boundary Park.

WEDNESDAY 22ND JUNE 1983

Goalkeeper Andy Gorton signed amateur forms, turning professional in 1985. Although he was on the books for around five years he only made 26 league starts. His chances were limited by being an understudy to Andy Goram, but when Goram joined Hibernian, Gorton should have grasped his chance. Unfortunately, his off-field antics led to him being transfer listed.

MONDAY 23RD JUNE 1924

Centre-forward William Fergusson was signed by Reading for £100. He was signed by Oldham in January 1923 after hitting 35 goals in a season at Sunbeam Motor Works. He found the competition tough at Boundary Park but became the Royals' leading marksman in the 1924/25 season.

MONDAY 23RD JUNE 1952

Athletic transferred Tom Johnston to Norwich City for a fee of £500. Johnston was an old-time bustling centre-forward who only played five league games for Oldham, although he came to prominence with the Canaries and became their all-time leading goalscorer with 121 strikes.

THURSDAY 24TH JUNE 1897

Leslie Adlam was born in Guildford. Adlam made his Athletic debut in a home First Division game against Newcastle United, a 0-0 draw, on 30th March 1923. He cost Athletic £300 when he signed from Guildford United and was originally used as a centre-forward, though he also served the club well as a full-back. He scored 10 goals in 290 games for the club.

SATURDAY 24TH JUNE 1967

Goals from Ian Towers, Ian Wood and Eric Magee were enough to give the Latics a 3-1 win over FAR XI in Bulawayo on their Rhodesian tour.

SUNDAY 25TH JUNE 1967

Athletic's tour of Rhodesia and Malawi continued with a 4-2 victory against Dynamos in Salisbury. The attendance was 4,200 and the Latics goalscorers were Anthony Foster, Alan Hunter, Reg Blore and Bill Asprey (pen).

TUESDAY 26TH JUNE 1934

Outside-left Bill Hasson left Athletic to join Millwall after having scored 21 times in 135 league games. The Latics had signed him from Clyde for £150 which represented a great deal for a player with undoubted dribbling skill and exceptional ball control. Hasson died in 1976.

THURSDAY 27TH JUNE 1935

Billy Johnston left the Latics to take on the player-manager role at Frickley Colliery. Athletic had paid Manchester United £300 for the inside-forward in 1932. Johnston scored seven goals in his 64 league appearances.

FRIDAY 27TH JUNE 1958

Athletic paid Manchester City £250 for the services of Albert Bourne, a bustling inside-forward. He started his career well at Oldham but faded mid-season and was released at the end of the 1959/60 campaign having scored nine goals in 35 league appearances.

WEDNESDAY 28TH JUNE 1967

Mangula FC were the opposition for Athletic as they continued their tour of Rhodesia and Malawi. The Latics were too good for their counterparts and they ran out 4-0 winners with a hat-trick from Ian Wood and another strike from Ken Knighton.

SUNDAY 28TH JUNE 1992

Centre-half Tommy Williamson passed away in South Lowestoft. Signed from Northwich Victoria, he became the first post-war captain of the Latics and scored four goals in 169 appearances for the Blues. He attracted around 22,000 supporters for his benefit match against a star-studded 'International XI' which included Stanley Matthews, Stan Mortensen, Frank Swift and George Hardwick. Gate receipts were £1,149 and Williamson was awarded the maximum allowed at the time of £750. He retired to take up a business in Fleetwood.

WEDNESDAY 29TH JUNE 1949

Colin Garwood was born in Heacham, Norfolk and was a popular member of the Third Division promotion winning team of 1973/74. He scored some important goals for the club and hit a total of 36 in 92 league appearances.

TUESDAY 29TH JUNE 1965

Barrie Martin was transferred to Tranmere Rovers for a fee of £4,000. The classy defender had signed from Blackpool and scored four goals in 42 league appearances for the Latics. When Oldham paid £10,000 to the Seasiders for Martin, it was the club's second-highest transfer fee ever paid.

SUNDAY 30TH JUNE 1946

Alan Hunter was born at Sion Mills, County Tyrone in Ireland. He was given his league chance at Athletic in 1967 after being released by Leeds United. He was brought to Boundary Park along with several other Irishmen under the guidance of then manager Jimmy McIlroy. He went on to become an accomplished defender who appeared 83 times in the league, scoring a solitary goal.

OLDHAM ATHLETIC
On This Day

JULY

SATURDAY 1st JULY 1967

The Latics romped to an emphatic 7-3 victory in Rhodesia against Great Dykes Association XI in a game played in Mtoroshanga. Anthony Foster netted six times in the match which was played in front of 6,300 spectators. A penalty from Ken Knighton completed the scoring for the visitors. A second game was played on this day in Salisbury with Tornados as the opposition. The Latics came away with a 3-2 victory thanks to strikes from Ian Towers, Alan Hunter and an own goal.

WEDNESDAY 1st JULY 1992

Joe Royle made his record signing when he brought Ian Olney from Aston Villa to Boundary Park for a deal worth £700,000. Olney played 56 games for Oldham and scored 14 times.

SUNDAY 2nd JULY 1967

Athletic continued their Rhodesia and Malawi tour with another win. The result this time was 2-1 in a match against Manicaland XI in Umtali. Reg Blore and Anthony Foster were the scorers before a crowd of approximately 15,000.

SUNDAY 3rd JULY 1955

Jim Branagan, son of Ken, was born in Barton. He was a consistent full-back who followed in his father's footsteps. He regularly stepped in to cover for regular full-backs Ian Wood and Maurice Whittle and was also a mainstay of the Latics reserve side. He went on to make quite a name for himself as a Blackburn Rovers player and rarely missed a game in his nine seasons at Ewood Park.

THURSDAY 3rd JULY 1975

Gritty midfielder Alan McNeill left Athletic to join neighbours Stockport County after some sterling service for the Latics. He was a member of the Third Division championship-winning side and played in 169 league games for Athletic. An attack-minded player with a great shot, McNeill scored 19 league goals for the Blues.

TUESDAY 4th JULY 1899

The Black Cow Inn on Burnley Lane was the venue of a meeting where Oldham Athletic Association Football Club was born. The new club replaced the old Pine Villa – so named after the Pine Mill – and applied to join the Manchester Alliance League. The Latics were formed from a good squad of amateur players who just went from strength to strength!

MONDAY 4th JULY 1938

Goalkeeper Harry Dowd was born in Salford and went on to establish himself as a big favourite at Boundary Park. He made his debut at Northampton on December 5th 1970 in a Fourth Division fixture and conceded one goal in a 3-1 victory. Renowned for his unorthodox style of dribbling his way out of danger in the penalty box, Dowd made 121 league starts for the Latics. He was one of the few keepers to score a goal from open play, a feat he performed for Manchester City in the 1963/64 season.

FRIDAY 4th JULY 1958

Carl Valentine was born in Clayton. Valentine started as a 17-year-old with the Latics, making 82 league appearances and scoring 8 goals. He caught the eye of Vancouver Whitecaps' Tony Waiters, who signed him to help spark the club. After a stint back in England with West Bromwich Albion, Carl returned to Canada and played for his new country and helped them reach the 1986 World Cup finals for the first time. Carl continued as the Vancouver 86ers' player-manager, retiring in 1999. Since then he has been coaching youth soccer in North Vancouver. He was elected to the Canadian Soccer League's Player Hall of Fame in 2003.

SUNDAY 4th JULY 1967

Salisbury Callies entertained Athletic in Salisbury. A hat-trick from Keith Bebbington and goals from Ian Towers and Ian Wood gave the touring blues a 5-2 victory.

SUNDAY 4TH JULY 1982

Former Everton star Joe Royle was appointed manager to succeed the recently dispensed Jimmy Frizzell. The 33-year-old was quoted as saying, "Athletic are not a fashionable club, but success makes you fashionable – and that's what we are aiming for". It took a long time for Royle to become established, and fans would continue to sing the name of dethroned Jimmy Frizzell for many games into Royle's era. At the time, no one would have thought that he would go on to be Athletic's most successful manager of all time.

MONDAY 5TH JULY 1948

Stalwart Maurice Whittle was born in Wigan. Signed as a wing-half from Blackburn Rovers on 15th May 1959, Whittle only established himself after converting to full-back. He had a devastating left foot and scored 41 goals, many of them from dead-ball situations. The 'Chaddy End' used to cry "Maurice, Maurice" every time he stepped up to take a free kick, usually in anticipation of a forthcoming goal. He was a member of two promotion-winning teams and made a total of 343 appearances before moving on to Fort Lauderdale Strikers in the NASL.

WEDNESDAY 6TH JULY 1921

More than 40,000 people were shoe-horned into Boundary Park, one of the best crowds ever seen at the stadium. They were ex-servicemen, disabled soldiers, factory workers and schoolchildren who had gone to see HRH the Prince of Wales.

TUESDAY 6TH JULY 1967

Malawi FA lost 3-2 to the Latics in their penultimate game of their Rhodesia and Malawi tour. The Latics scorers were Eric Magee, Ian Towers and Reg Blore.

WEDNESDAY 7TH JULY 1965

Jim Pennington joined Athletic from Grimsby Town in a £2,000 deal. He was an outside-right who was tricky on the ball but rarely scored goals. After 23 league appearances he moved on to Rochdale and then Northwich Victoria.

WEDNESDAY 7th JULY 1971

Southport signed Barry Hartle. Originally a winger, he was converted to a full-back role at Stockport County. When the Latics tried to switch him back on the wing he found it difficult to break into a team that was on its way to winning promotion to Division Three, so he moved on after about a year – to Southport – in which he played in nine league games and got two goals.

THURSDAY 8th JULY 1965

Ray Holt, a 25-year-old half-back, was signed by Gordon Hurst from Huddersfield Town for a fee of £3,000. He did not figure much in manager Jimmy McIlroy's plans and failed to make his first appearance until the middle of the 1965/66 season. He played only 14 league games and scored one goal although he subsequently gave good service to Halifax Town and Scunthorpe United.

SATURDAY 8th JULY 1967

Athletic rounded off their tour of Rhodesia and Malawi with a resounding 6-2 victory at Blantyre Sports Club. Anthony Foster was on the mark again with a hat-trick, while Ian Towers chipped in with two and Ian Wood completed the scoring. The attendance was around 3,000. Foster was the hero of the tour hitting a total of 11 goals.

TUESDAY 9th JULY 1957

Ted West joined Athletic from Gillingham. He was a reliable full-back and for the next three seasons he made the position his own, appearing in 117 league games. He was released in 1961 and went to ply his trade in Australia for Bankstown FC.

WEDNESDAY 9th JULY 1969

Inside-forward Eric Magee moved to Port Vale. Athletic had picked him up at the age of 15 from Glenavon reserves and he first played for the Latics on their tour of Rhodesia and Malawi in 1967. He went on to make 45 league appearances and score nine goals before joining the Burslem side.

MONDAY 9TH JULY 1984

Full-back Willie Donachie was signed from Burnley and became player-coach in 1985. He then progressed to become Joe Royle's right-hand man and shared in the successful team that Royle built. He played on into the veteran stage but always gave 100% in everything he did and was always a credit to the club.

MONDAY 10TH JULY 1899

There was an official announcement in the *Oldham Standard* which reported: "The Pine Villa AFC has secured the Oldham Athletic Grounds and the club will be known in future as the Oldham Athletic Club."

THURSDAY 11TH JULY 1935

Goalkeeper Johnny Bollands was born in Middlesbrough. He was a quick and decisive stopper who had two spells with the club between 1953 and 1966. He made a total of 154 league appearances and was an England under-23 international.

SATURDAY 11TH JULY 1936

Bill Marshall was born in Belfast. Signed from Burnley, he only played six senior games in his time at Turf Moor but he was a regular member of the Latics side who won promotion in his first season.

SATURDAY 11TH JULY 1970

Athletic paid Preston North End £6,000 for no-nonsense wing-half Bill Cranston. Manager Jimmy Frizzell had no hesitation in making him team captain and he led the club to promotion to Division Three in his first season at the club. The defence-minded player clocked up a century of league games for the Latics, scoring two goals in the process.

SATURDAY 12TH JULY 2003

A celebrity match was held at Boundary Park to raise funds for cash-strapped Athletic who were seriously in danger of ceasing to exist. It was organised by the newly formed Supporters' Trust and could have been the last ever match to be played at the ground. The players were led out by former boss Joe Royle and the game was a huge financial success.

THURSDAY 13TH JULY 1972

Much-travelled centre-forward Tony Hateley signed for Athletic. The big name capture caused quite a stir at the time as he was likened to the great Dixie Dean with his cavalier style. Great things were expected but Hateley only made one appearance, and four as substitute, grabbing a single goal. He failed to recover from a cartilage operation and retired from the game in May 1974.

TUESDAY 13TH JULY 1976

Mark Hilton became an apprentice and went on to turn professional in January 1978. He found it hard to establish himself in the first team and moved over to neighbours Bury. His career at Gigg Lane was ended when he broke his leg in a Lancashire County Cup game, ironically against Oldham Athletic, at Boundary Park in 1982.

THURSDAY 14TH JULY 2005

Athletic completed the signing of Luke Beckett from Sheffield United on a season-long loan deal. The striker had spent the final few weeks of the previous season at Boundary Park, and had helped the Latics to avoid relegation with six goals in nine games. After signing the deal, the 28-year-old said, "It has taken a long time but I am glad everything is finally sorted out". His second loan period ended in May 2006.

TUESDAY 15TH JULY 1924

Reliable full-back Teddy Ivill joined the Latics from Atherton. A 'Mr Consistency' who never missed a match in five full seasons, he was a true stalwart who notched up a total of 277 league games and two goals. He was rightfully awarded a benefit game against Barnsley at Boundary Park in May 1932.

TUESDAY 15TH JULY 1958

Centre-forward Reuben Butler died in Heworth, County Durham. He was a big and burly striker who led the Latics goalscoring charts in the 1920/21 and 1921/22 seasons. He scored on his debut at Middlesbrough on 28th August 1920 and notched a total of 34 goals in his 77 league appearances.

TUESDAY 16TH JULY 1918

Peter McKennan was born in Airdrie. He was signed by player-manager George Hardwick for £3,000 and helped Athletic win the Third Division (North) championship after his inspirational play motivated the team. He scored 33 goals in his 83 appearances for the Latics. He left in July 1954 to join Coleraine as player/coach. Peter died in Dundonald, Ayrshire in October 1991.

THURSDAY 17TH JULY 1919

Archie Whyte was born in Redding, Stirlingshire. He was signed from Barnsley as part of a double deal that also brought Ernie Swallow to Boundary Park. Whyte was a major player in the Third Division (North) championship winning side of 1952-53 and his defensive qualities had a huge bearing on the Latics' success. He made 100 consecutive appearances and retired in June 1956 when he was appointed assistant trainer until he was replaced by Henry Cockburn in 1960. Having made 248 appearances for Athletic, Archie died on 1st October 1973 in Middleton.

THURSDAY 17TH JULY 1958

Norman Dodgin was appointed as manager of Athletic, taking over from Ted Goodier. Dodgin was 37 and one of the youngest managers in football. He gained a reputation for taking young players and moulding them into good ones. Dodgin was quoted; "Football is such an up and down game that one can only give it everything you've got, and I will certainly do that".

SATURDAY 18TH JULY 1896

Alderman Thomas Bolton, who later became Mayor of the Borough, cut the first sod on what was to be the Latics' new ground at Boundary Park. Alderman Bolton was presented with the commemorative spade with which he cut the earth. The spade is engraved: "Presented to Alderman Thomas Bolton, Oldham. County Association Football & Athletic Club, on the occasion of cutting the first sod of their New Ground at Westhulme, Oldham, July 18th 1896". The spade is now on display at Boundary Park.

TUESDAY 19th JULY 1960

A heated meeting was held at the King Street Baptist Church as over 300 shareholders packed the room. Seven new directors were appointed to the Athletic board, but it was a controversial vote with claims that the proxy poll was invalid.

SATURDAY 20th JULY 1957

Tommy Walker signed for a second spell at Boundary Park. He was a Methodist lay preacher who could play on either wing. He retired in April 1959 to take charge of a newsagent in nearby Middleton.

FRIDAY 20th JULY 1962

'Big Jim' Bowie made the trip south from Arthurlie Juniors to sign for Athletic. Bought to replace the great Bobby Johnstone, he was never going to fill those boots. The tall Scotsman soon became a popular figure with the Latics fans as he used his 6ft 2ins height to great effect. He completed a ten-year stay at Boundary Park, making 334 league appearances and scoring 38 league goals.

WEDNESDAY 20th JULY 1966

Midfield/defender Ronnie Blair signed for Athletic as an amateur, becoming a professional in October of the same year. Blair had two spells at Oldham and was always a firm favourite with the fans. He played in the Division Three championship side and also won five caps for Northern Ireland in a distinguished career.

SATURDAY 20th JULY 1968

Forward Ian Towers left Athletic to join local club Bury. He had a good return of goals while at the Latics with 45 being scored in 95 league appearances.

WEDNESDAY 21st JULY 1926

Inside-forward Bob Gillespie left Athletic to sign for Luton Town. He was originally spotted playing for Newton Heath Loco and the 5ft 7ins player first made his debut for the Latics as an amateur. Gillespie was released on a free transfer after Athletic brought in new signings of the calibre of Albert Pynegar, Arthur Ormston and Horace Barnes.

THURSDAY 22ND JULY 1965

Stewart Holden signed from Huddersfield Town. The 23-year-old utility midfielder had his best spell for the Latics as a full-back. It was probably his versatility that prevented him from establishing a permanent spot in the team but he managed to record 42 league games for the Blues and scored six goals. He was also an accomplished cricket player who played for local team Heyside for several years.

THURSDAY 23RD JULY 1959

Half-back Brian Jarvis arrived at Boundary Park after being signed from Wrexham. He made his debut at home in a Fourth Division game against Bradford City on 22nd August in a 2-0 win. Peter Stringfellow got both goals. Jarvis was a gutsy player who gave great service to the Latics and he went on to make 88 league appearances for the 'boys in Blue', scoring two goals. He was rewarded in his final season with a promotion-winning medal.

WEDNESDAY 23RD JULY 1975

Long-time defender Gary Hoolickin signed a professional contract after serving as an apprentice since 9th April 1974. His debut came at home to Luton Town on 14th May 1977 in a Second Division match that Athletic lost 2-1. He had a long career at Boundary Park and was rewarded with a testimonial game against Manchester City on 9th September 1986.

MONDAY 24TH JULY 1939

Arthur Bailey joined Athletic from Stalybridge Celtic for a second spell at Boundary Park. He also went on to be a regular wartime player and made a total of 137 appearances and scored 52 goals between 1939 and 1945. Bailey was also a joiner by trade.

TUESDAY 24TH JULY 1951

Inside-forward Peter McKennan signed from Middlesbrough. His inspirational play was a great asset to the team and he was the type of player who always wanted to be a 'winner'. He scored 28 goals in 78 league games and also represented the Scottish League XI on two occasions.

FRIDAY 25TH JULY 2003

A management buy-out team, led by marketing boss Sean Jarvis and club accountant Neil Joy, became the new owners of Oldham Athletic after owner Chris Moore cruelly revealed that he was pulling everything out of the club. Moore agreed to sell his 95 per cent stake for just £1 and also agreed to write off £4.5m owed to him by the club after announcing that he was no longer willing to bankroll the Latics. Just days after, irate fans burned his effigy outside his business HQ in Banbury after players were sold off and manager Iain Dowie had been left with just 12 professionals.

THURSDAY 26TH JULY 1979

Leicester City paid a whopping £250,000 to take Alan Young to Filbert Street. The purchase was fueled by the hat-trick that the youngster had notched against them in a fourth round FA Cup tie in 1979. It proved a good deal for all concerned as Athletic had got him for nothing... and for his 14 goals that helped Leicester to the Second Division championship.

SATURDAY 27TH JULY 1918

Lewis Brook was born in Halifax and made his Athletic debut in a Third Division (North) 0-0 home draw with Lincoln City on 13th March 1948. He played in 196 games for the Latics and scored 14 goals. He lost his front line spot to Eric Gemmell in the 1948/49 season but scored 19 goals for the reserves in 22 matches. He regained his first team position and was converted to right-back in George Hardwick's championship-winning team at the age of 34.

SUNDAY 27TH JULY 1930

Stalwart Ken Branagan was born in Salford. Branagan joined Athletic as a 30-year-old in a double deal with Bert Lister from Manchester City in 1960 for a fee of £10,000. The full-back went on to make 195 appearances with five goals in his six-year stay at Boundary Park.

THURSDAY 28TH JULY 1966

Ian Wood signed as a professional for Athletic having joined the Oldham as an amateur some eight months earlier from Park Lane Olympic. Ian went on to make a record number of appearances for the Latics over many years, making the right-back position his own.

SATURDAY 29TH JULY 1978

A benefit game was held at Boundary Park between Oldham Athletic and Blackpool. The match was to raise funds for the dependents of Alan Groves who tragically died of a heart attack at the age of just 29. Groves had been a popular performer and was one of those players who just had to 'entertain' the fans. A crowd of 4,396 showed up to pay their last respects to a great player who had given his all to both clubs.

TUESDAY 30TH JULY 1957

A fee of £400 was needed to bring Bill Farmer to Athletic from Loughborough. Signed as a goalkeeper to replace Derek Williams, who had been sent overseas with the forces, he had a terrible record in his first five games. He let in 13 goals and did not play again as David Teece took over the role. Farmer moved on to Worcester City in July 1958.

SUNDAY 31ST JULY 1887

Tommy Broad was born in Stalybridge. He had amazing speed and was recognised as the most dangerous winger in the country. He made his Second Division debut at Birmingham City on 4th September 1909 in a 2-2 draw and was a member of the team that won promotion to the First Division. His final game for Oldham was in a little-known-about Austrian tour in 1911. He played against Wiener Sporting Club in Vienna and was then transferred to Bristol City for £6,000 after scoring nine goals in 104 games for the Latics. Tommy died in 1966 at Barton Irwell.

OLDHAM ATHLETIC
On This Day

AUGUST

FRIDAY 1st AUGUST 1980

Blond-haired defender Paul Futcher signed from Manchester City for a fee of £150,000. He was a skilful player with good vision and became one of the best defenders in the Second Division. He made 98 league starts for the Latics and scored one goal.

THURSDAY 1st AUGUST 1991

Manager Joe Royle signed striker Graeme Sharp from Everton in a £500,000 deal. Sharp later went on to manage the club. Also on this day, defender Brian Kilcline was signed from Coventry City for a fee of £400,000. He made a paltry 10 appearances before being sold on to Newcastle United for £250,000.

TUESDAY 2nd AUGUST 1960

Manager Jack Rowley was appointed. The former Manchester United and England international player was the type who would command respect and said, "It is too early for me to make any predictions for the future, but it will be my aim to put a team on the field which tries to play football. I have no time for kick and rush tactics."

He was responsible for bringing players like Bobby Johnstone, Ken Branagan, Bert Lister and Bob Rackley to Oldham in his first year. They all made their debuts in a memorable season after so many years of preceding doom and gloom. Rowley's team went on a run of ten successive victories but they finished a respectable 12th place in the Fourth Division after a poor start.

WEDNESDAY 3rd AUGUST 1966

Goalkeeper Gary Kelly was born at Fulwood near Preston. He came from a goalkeeping family as his father Alan played 447 games for Preston North End and his brother, also named Alan, appeared in goal for five league clubs. Gary appeared in a total of 265 games for Athletic, joining from neighbours Bury for a fee of £10,000 in 1996 and spending six years at Boundary Park eventually leaving in 2003 to join Northwich Victoria.

WEDNESDAY 4TH AUGUST 1943

Keith Bebbington was born in Cuddington, near Nantwich and played at Boundary Park between 1966 and 1972, racking up an impressive 255 appearances, scoring 46 goals. Bebbington was a tricky winger who could operate equally as well in the inside-right position. He served under three mangers at Oldham; Jimmy McIlroy, Jack Rowley and Jimmy Frizzell. Bebbington later moved to Rochdale in exchange for Ronnie Blair.

WEDNESDAY 5TH AUGUST 1942

Dick Mulvaney was born in Sunderland. He was snapped up on a free transfer from Blackburn Rovers after being in dispute, and was made club captain of the 1973/74 Third Division championship-winning side. One of the most consistent centre-backs of that era, he helped the Latics establish themselves in the Second Division. Dick got two goals in his 92 league appearances for the club.

THURSDAY 6TH AUGUST 1959

One of the youngest players to sign professional in the early years died in Werneth. Arthur Gee scored 46 goals in 119 games for Athletic between 1911 and 1921. He represented Athletic in the First Division and his weekly pay was £4. The England schoolboy international, a strong and gritty individual, joined the club from Earlstown for a fee of £30. David Ashworth negotiated the signing after watching him play against Eccles Borough in the Lancashire Combination. He left the Latics for Stalybridge Celtic for their first season in the newly-formed Third Division (North).

SATURDAY 6TH AUGUST 2005

Yeovil Town travelled to Boundary Park for their first-ever game at League One level but were soon bounced back down to earth after their heroics of the previous season, when they were crowned champions of League Two. Chris Porter and Paul Warne scored a goal each in the first half to give Athletic a 2-0 win in front of 6,979 fans.

SATURDAY 7TH AUGUST 1999

Preston North End beat Athletic 1-0 in the opening match of the new season in this Division Two game at Boundary Park. Jon Macken got the only goal of the game in the 65th minute.

SATURDAY 7TH AUGUST 2004

Will Haining put Athletic ahead after 10 minutes in the opening fixture of League One at a sunny Kenilworth Road. The Hatters fought back though, and goals from Howard and Underwood gave the home side all the points.

SATURDAY 8TH AUGUST 1998

A 3-1 Division Two home defeat to Notts County was hardly the start to the season that Athletic had expected. The win put County top of the league. The Latics were comprehensively beaten and the last minute goal by Andy Holt was nothing more than a consolation.

TUESDAY 8TH AUGUST 2006

John Sheridan was still looking for his team's first point in League One after taking over as manager from Ronnie Moore in June. After a loss at Tranmere Rovers, Port Vale brought their team to Boundary Park and a Sodje goal in the 66th minute was sufficient for them to return home with all three points.

WEDNESDAY 9TH AUGUST 1933

British record transfer Albert Quixall was born in Sheffield. He found fame with Manchester United and it was a feather in the cap for Athletic to bring him to Boundary Park for the miserly sum of £8,500. He was bought to halt the slump that the Latics were going through in 1964, but the supporters never saw the best of the undoubted skills that he possessed due to persistent injuries.

MONDAY 9TH AUGUST 1954

Latics stalwart Keith Hicks was born in Oldham. Hicks was a popular defender and good in the air. He made his debut at the tender age of 17. In his ten years at Boundary Park he scored 12 goals in 269 appearances. He was also an England youth international and was a member of the 1973/74 Third Division championship-winning team.

MONDAY 9th AUGUST 1993

Defender-cum-striker Ian Marshall signed for Ipswich Town for £750,000. Marshall had done sterling work for Athletic in both his roles. Even he was not sure whether he should be a defender or a striker but the Latics fans who were around at the time will fondly remember his very important goals as well as his match-saving tackles.

TUESDAY 9th AUGUST 1994

Record-breaking Frankie Bunn enjoyed a testimonial game against Everton at Boundary Park. Just six months after his finest hour, his career lay in ruins after a knee injury, which finished him off at the tender age of 27.

SATURDAY 10th AUGUST 2002

Athletic slumped to their first opening day defeat of the new millennium in a Division Two loss to Cardiff City. The Welshmen sneaked a 2-1 away win in a match that saw Iain Dowie give a debut to Sporting Lisbon's loanee Lourenco. Lee Duxbury got the Latics' consolation goal in the 90th minute.

WEDNESDAY 11th AUGUST 1965

Norwegian international Gunnar Halle was born in Larvik, Norway. He signed a three-year contract with Athletic in January 1991 and manager Joe Royle saw him as a replacement for the popular Paul Warhurst in the Latics' surge to promotion from the Second Division. Halle suffered a cracked fibula in the 7-1 hammering of Torquay United in the League Cup and another injury in December put him out for the season. He came back to play in the First Division with the Latics and at the time was the club's most capped player. Halle left to join Leeds United in December 1996 for £400,000 after making 212 appearances for Oldham, scoring 21 goals.

SATURDAY 11th AUGUST 2007

Oldham gave debuts to Michael Ricketts and Craig Davies in a League One 2-1 home win over Swansea City. Ricketts was brought down in the penalty area and stepped up to convert in the third minute. Davies popped up with a 90th minute winner.

SATURDAY 12TH AUGUST 1995

Athletic hammered Huddersfield Town 3-0 in the Division One opening match of the new season. The Latics scorers were Stuart Barlow, Carl Serrant and Lee Richardson.

SATURDAY 12TH AUGUST 2006

Chris Howarth made his debut for Athletic when he stepped in goal for the injured Les Pogliacomi. Simon Charlton also made his debut in the League One home fixture against Swansea City. Maheta Molango got the only goal of the game to give the Latics a victory. The 20-year-old Howarth made himself an instant hero when he saved a badly-taken penalty from Lee Trundle to deny the Swans anything from the game.

SATURDAY 13TH AUGUST 1969

Athletic bowed out of the League Cup at the first round stage when they lost 5-1 at Southport. With less than 3,000 fans at Haig Avenue, Derek Spence got the lone goal for the visitors.

SATURDAY 13TH AUGUST 1994

Charlton Athletic were the visitors for the opening First Division (second tier) game of the season. The Latics went wild and a 5-2 victory saw them sitting proudly at the top of the table, albeit after only one game! Sean McCarthy and Lee Richardson got two goals each and Graeme Sharp notched the other.

WEDNESDAY 14TH AUGUST 1985

The first of a series of deals that manager Joe Royle was to make his trademark occurred. He sold Mark Ward to West Ham United and made a £240,000 profit for the club.

SATURDAY 14TH AUGUST 1993

Ipswich Town left Boundary Park with all three points in the first Premiership match of the season. The 3-0 drubbing that they handed out was sufficient to leave the Latics floundering at the bottom of the league.

SATURDAY 14TH AUGUST 2004

Walsall were beaten 5-3 in a thriller at Oldham in League One. The Saddlers were still coming to terms with the division following relegation.

TUESDAY 14TH AUGUST 2007

In torrential rain, Athletic brushed aside Mansfield Town in this League Cup game at Boundary Park. Ex-Latics player Billy Dearden brought his team along hoping to cause an upset but it wasn't a happy return as the Latics won 4-1. Dean Smalley scored his first senior goal for the club and summer signings Neil Kilkenny and Jean-Paul Kalala both found the back of the net. Craig Davies completed the rout with his second goal in two outings.

SATURDAY 15TH AUGUST 1970

The opening match of the Fourth Division season was at Grimsby Town and Athletic gave debuts to Maurice Short, Bill Cranston, Don Heath and Barry Hartle. The game didn't go the Latics way, though, as they lost the encounter 4-1 with Jimmy Fryatt getting the only Athletic goal.

SATURDAY 15TH AUGUST 1992

Chelsea were the visitors to Boundary Park for Athletic's first season in the newly-formed Premier League and 20,699 spectators were present to witness the momentous event. Mick Harford had given the Pensioners the lead and it looked like an inaugural defeat for the Latics, but Nick Henry popped in an 86th minute equaliser to give the home side a share of the points. Steve Redmond made his debut for Athletic.

THURSDAY 16TH AUGUST 1945

Alan McNeill was born in Belfast. One of Athletic's best midfielders, he joined the club in October 1969. McNeill was an influential character who helped the club to win the Third Division championship in the 1973/74 season. McNeill scored 19 times for the Latics and appeared in 185 games before he left to join Stockport County in July 1975.

SATURDAY 16TH AUGUST 1969

Newport County were the visitors for a Fourth Division game in which Athletic ran out easy 3-0 winners. Jim Beardall got two goals and Les Chapman scored the other, although less than 5,000 fans turned up to see the spectacle.

SATURDAY 16th AUGUST 2003

Athletic made the short trip to Hillsborough to take on Sheffield Wednesday in this Division Two clash. The pre-match talk in the pubs was about the return of former Owls hero John Sheridan and whether he would be playing. Still revered in Sheffield, he certainly made his mark in the game as quickly as the sixth minute when he scored from the penalty spot to put the Latics ahead.

The former Wednesday legend dominated the play from midfield in a match where manager Iain Dowie had instilled the winning mentality to his team. Both teams had a player sent off – Danny Hall was the Latics player to walk. Antoine-Curier got the equalising goal to give the visitors a creditable 2-2 draw, witnessed by 24,160 supporters in the Steel City.

SATURDAY 17th AUGUST 1991

The Latics played their first Division One game for 68 years when they travelled to Anfield for the opening match of the season. Earl Barrett scored the first goal at this level, since the last time they graced the top flight, in the eighth minute of the game. Liverpool went on to win 2-1 but Athletic were back!

SATURDAY 18th AUGUST 1962

Bradford City were welcomed to Boundary Park for the opening fixture of a new Fourth Division season. Bob Ledger made his debut in a game that Athletic won 2-1. Bert Lister opened the scoring within two minutes and debut boy Ledger added the winner in the second half.

SATURDAY 19th AUGUST 1950

Rotherham United were the first team to visit Boundary Park for the opening Third Division (North) game in the 1950/51 season. A crowd of 19,182 watched Archie Whyte, Ernie Swallow and goalkeeper George Bradshaw make their debuts. The game was a nine-goal thriller with the Latics losing out by the odd goal. Haddington got two goals, one a penalty, while Munro and Ormond got the other markers.

WEDNESDAY 19TH AUGUST 1953

Athletic played their opening match back in the Second Division after having won promotion the previous season. The result was an amazing 4-4 draw at Luton Town. However, life was tough at their new level and they failed to win a match until their ninth game when they beat Lincoln City 1-0.

TUESDAY 19TH AUGUST 2003

An administration order was granted against Oldham at the High Court of Justice Chancery Division in the Leeds District Registry. The move came three weeks before they faced another court appearance, which could have ended in bankruptcy. Manchester-based administrators PKF moved into Boundary Park to run the club as a going concern: the club had debts of £2.9m and were losing a staggering £50,000 per week. Athletic were given six weeks to raise £500,000 to ensure the Football League that the season's fixtures could be completed.

SATURDAY 20TH AUGUST 1960

Jimmy Frizzell, Jimmy Rollo and Kevin McCurley all made their debuts in the home Fourth Division fixture against Northampton Town. The Latics lost 2-1 in a game where McCurley had to be carried off after 43 minutes. Unfortunately, he never played for Athletic again.

SATURDAY 20TH AUGUST 1966

Leyton Orient were the visitors for the first game of a new Third Division season in which Keith Bebbington made his debut. Athletic won 3-1 with a penalty from Bill Asprey and two goals from Frank Large.

WEDNESDAY 21ST AUGUST 1991

The first home match in Division One for 68 years saw Chelsea visit Boundary Park and the home fans were treated to a goal feast as Athletic saw off the Londoners with a convincing 3-0 scoreline.

TUESDAY 22ND AUGUST 1922

On this day in Stoke-on-Trent, John McCue was born. He made a great full-back partnership with Ken Branagan after he had signed from Stoke City in 1960 at the age of 38. He made 56 league appearances in his two-year stay at Boundary Park.

SUNDAY 22ND AUGUST 1954

Goalkeeper John Platt was born in Ashton-under-Lyne. He made 109 first team league starts for the Latics before sustaining an injury which sidelined him for good. He was appointed stadium manager in 1986 and went on to supervise the Football in the Community programme at Boundary Park.

WEDNESDAY 22ND AUGUST 2001

An era ended when Bobby Johnstone passed away in Selkirk, aged 71. Johnstone will be fondly remembered as Athletic's biggest-ever crowd-puller and best-loved entertainer. He was the master craftsman of his trade; clever on the ball, a supreme footballing artist, a talented exponent of the weighted pass and a player who, with one sway of the hips, would often leave defenders literally going the wrong way.

After a memorable career with Hibs (twice) and Manchester City – with whom he made history in 1955 and 1956 by becoming the first player to score in successive Wembley FA Cup finals – Johnstone was brought to Oldham by Jack Rowley in the autumn of 1960.

He was so accurate that his penalty kicks invariably went in off the post. His debut game for the club attracted 17,116 spectators. He was an instant success and scored 37 goals in 158 games. Without him there would be no Oldham Athletic in existence today. He was that important to the club!

SUNDAY 23RD AUGUST 1964

Goalkeeper Andy Rhodes was born in Doncaster. Even though he only played in 11 league games for the Latics, Rhodes was a spectacular keeper who made many great saves after adapting to the then artificial turf of Boundary Park. He only appeared in one defeat for the Latics and went on to be a goalkeeping coach at the club.

TUESDAY 23RD AUGUST 2005

The Latics bowed out of the first round of the League Cup with hardly a whimper to a strong Leeds United side. The 2-0 loss was watched by 14,970 at Elland Road.

SATURDAY 24TH AUGUST 1957

The first Third Division (North) match of the season was at home to Carlisle United and a crowd of 11,339 saw two players make their second 'debut' for the club. Bill Spurdle had just returned to Boundary Park after a spell at Port Vale and Tommy Walker was back from a time at Chesterfield. Spurdle scored the only goal of the game to give the Latics a winning start.

FRIDAY 24TH AUGUST 1990

Midfielder and crowd favourite Mike Milligan was sold to Everton in a £1m deal. Milligan had been at Boundary Park since his apprenticeship and only stayed at Goodison Park for a year before returning to Athletic in a £600,000 move. In his two spells at Oldham he played a massive 336 games and scored 27 goals.

SATURDAY 24TH AUGUST 2002

Clint Hill scored his first goal for Athletic in a 2-0 win over his former club Tranmere Rovers. A crowd of 5,933 witnessed the Latics get their win while inflicting the first Division Two defeat of the season on the visitors. The game also saw the debut of Clyde Wijnhard, who also scored when he volleyed home a Carlo Corazzin flick.

TUESDAY 24TH AUGUST 2004

Stoke City brought their undefeated Championship team to Boundary Park for a League Cup first round tie. In a game that was decided with controversial refereeing decisions, the visitors took the lead through Carl Asaba but the Latics fought back to win with goals from David Eyres and a disputed penalty after ex-Latics player Clint Hill was adjudged to have handled a Jermain Johnston shot. John Eyre converted the spot kick in front of a disappointing gate of 2,861.

SATURDAY 25TH AUGUST 1945

The war was over. Athletic kicked off a new season in the Third Division (North) West Region League against Crewe. Boundary Park had been cleared of wartime debris and was newly whitewashed.

SATURDAY 25TH AUGUST 1984

Neil Adams and Willie Donachie both made their debuts for Athletic in the home game against Birmingham City. An own goal by Kenny Clements was enough to give Birmingham a win in their first season in the Second Division after being relegated.

MONDAY 25TH AUGUST 1986

The tail-end of a gale-force wind – typical Oldham weather – was the conditions that Athletic endured in the first-ever game to be played on the new artificial surface at Boundary Park. Rather than playing on a lush carpet, the fibrilated polypropolyne pitch looked more like a beach than a football field due to all the sand necessary to help it bed in. Gone was the famous slope of 6ft 4½, which used to decline down to the Chaddy End, as it had been levelled with the changes to the pitch. Barnsley were the visitors for the first Second Division home match of the new season and goals from Nick Henry and Roger Palmer were enough to see off the Yorkshire rivals.

SATURDAY 25TH AUGUST 1990

Molineux was the venue for the first Second Division match of the new season. Never an easy place to visit, the Latics travelled full of confidence and came away with a marvellous 3-2 victory. Ian Marshall, the converted centre-back, did the damage with a stunning hat-trick to silence the Wolves supporters.

SUNDAY 26TH AUGUST 1900

Bert Watson was born in Thelwell, Cheshire. After being rejected by Manchester United, he had a brief spell at Witton Albion before signing for Oldham for £300 and being given his league debut. He hit 72 goals in 242 appearances for the Latics in his eight-year stay, which was the highest total by any pre-war Athletic player. He scored twice in Athletic's record FA Cup win of 10-1 over Lytham and was transferred to Southampton in 1929. Bert died in January 1971 at Thelwell.

THURSDAY 26TH AUGUST 1926

Bill Ormond was born in Greenock. A winger who could play on either flank, he hit 25 goals in his 122 league games for Oldham before leaving the struggling Latics, who ended up rock bottom of the Second Division table in the 1953/54 season.

SATURDAY 26TH AUGUST 1933

Brian Jarvis was born at Bangor-on-Dee and signed for Athletic, from Wrexham, in 1959. An uncompromising wing-half, he featured in 88 league games for the club, scoring twice. He was fast and showed great ability in build-up play. His final season at Boundary Park was in the 1962/63 promotion year.

SATURDAY 26TH AUGUST 1939

Amidst air-raid warnings and Roosevelt's second peace appeal to Hitler, the Latics entertained Carlisle United in thundery conditions at Boundary Park. Oldham won the game 3-1 but the season had to be aborted as footballers' contracts were cancelled due to the war.

WEDNESDAY 26TH AUGUST 1961

Johnny Colquhoun, the diminutive inside-forward, was signed from Stirling Albion for a fee of £6,000. He went on to score many important goals for Athletic in his two stints at the club and was an ever-present in the promotion season of 1962/63, playing a total of 233 league games for the Blues, scoring 39 times. Colquhoun made his debut on the same day in the 2-2 home draw with Colchester United in a Fourth Division match watched by 15,746 supporters. Goals from Alan Shackleton and Bobby Johnstone earned a point, but left Athletic still looking for their first league win of the season.

SATURDAY 27TH AUGUST 1960

The trip to Bradford Park Avenue was very disappointing for the Latics, as they came home humiliated from a 5-1 mauling. The win left Bradford top of the Fourth Division. Over 9,000 fans watched the game in which Brian Birch got the only Latics goal from the penalty spot.

SATURDAY 27TH AUGUST 1994

Lancashire neighbours Burnley visited Boundary Park for a Division One game but went home with their tails between their legs after a 3-0 hammering. Over 11,000 people watched Sean McCarthy hit two goals while Andy Ritchie completed the scoring for the home side.

TUESDAY 28TH AUGUST 1990

Leicester City visited Athletic for the first home match of the Second Division season and goals from Ian Marshall and Andy Ritchie were enough to see off any challenge that the Foxes could muster. The game was unfortunate for club captain Andy Holden, who suffered a knee injury that was serious enough to keep him out of action for the remainder of the season.

THURSDAY 28TH AUGUST 2003

The Football League demanded that Athletic proved that they could continue their fixtures for the coming season, at a cost of over £1m. If they failed to do so by the next board meeting on 8th September, the league could suspend the Latics from playing any further Division Two matches.

MONDAY 29TH AUGUST 1988

The first away game of the Second Division campaign was an exciting prospect with a trip to local rivals Manchester City. The match couldn't have gone much better, as City old boy Roger Palmer tormented his former employers with a devastating display of finishing. He racked up a hat-trick as Athletic ran riot in a 4-1 victory.

MONDAY 30TH AUGUST 1920

A close-fought game with Blackburn Rovers resulted in a 1-0 home win for Athletic in this First Division fixture. Reuben Butler got the only goal of the game in front of 23,552 enthusiastic spectators.

THURSDAY 30TH AUGUST 1990

Hull City defender Richard Jobson was signed by manager Joe Royle in a deal worth £450,000. He went on to rack up 225 appearances for the Latics and scored 11 goals in a distinguished career at Boundary Park. He later signed for Leeds United in a £1m deal.

MONDAY 30TH AUGUST 1994

A 3-1 win at Notts County resulted in Athletic sitting atop the Division One table with nine points. The victory was achieved with the help of a Sean McCarthy hat-trick.

MONDAY 30TH AUGUST 2004

Around 2,000 Latics fans travelled over the Pennines to see the League One clash at Sheffield Wednesday. Chris Brunt put the Owls ahead in the 70th minute, much to the delight of the majority of the 21,530 spectators. Five minutes later it was the turn of the Athletic fans to cheer after a long clearance from Les Pogliacomi sent Jermain Johnson away to put the Latics level. The Wednesday were booed off the field at the end of the game. No such misery for the Blue Army, who were celebrating another step in the right direction.

SATURDAY 31ST AUGUST 1935

Athletic played their first game ever in the new surroundings of the Third Division (North) against Mansfield Town, going down 1-0. A club spokesman commented; "There is a greater dispersion in the Northern Section to make up for a lack of science with a little bit of extra vigour. Well, we are down, and when you are in Rome, you must do as Rome does. We shall have to play them at their own game".

SATURDAY 31ST AUGUST 1946

Over 7,000 spectators turned up to watch the return to regular football after the conclusion of World War II. Carlisle United were the opposition for the opening match of the Third Division (North) season at Boundary Park. The fans went home disappointed, though, as the Latics were defeated 2-0.

OLDHAM ATHLETIC
On This Day

SEPTEMBER

SATURDAY 1st SEPTEMBER 1906

Athletic played their first game at their new ground, Boundary Park. Colne were the visitors and 3,454 people paid £51 13s 6d to enter. Goals from David Walders and Harry Hancock gave Athletic a 2-0 win.

SATURDAY 1st SEPTEMBER 1990

A 3-1 home win over Portsmouth witnessed by 11,657 was enough to fire Athletic top of the Second Division. Goals from Rick Holden, Paul Warhurst and an own goal by Martin Kuhl did the damage.

SATURDAY 1st SEPTEMBER 2007

At the Victoria Ground, just over 5,000 watched Hartlepool United give Athletic a 4-1 thumping. Craig Davies got the consolation goal in a match that left the Latics in the relegation zone of League One.

SATURDAY 2nd SEPTEMBER 1899

The club played their first friendly game at Sheepfoot Lane under their new name of Oldham Athletic, having previously been known as Pine Villa. They entertained a team of shoe blackers called Berry's 'A' from the Lancashire Combination. Hernan scored the all important only goal of the game which gave them a 1-0 victory. The match lasted 80 minutes and was watched by approximately 1,000 fans.

MONDAY 2nd SEPTEMBER 1940

Big centre-forward Jimmy Fryatt was born in Swaythling, Southampton. Fryatt was the first signing by then caretaker manager, Jimmy Frizzell when he arrived from Blackburn Rovers for a fee of £8,000. His robust style soon made him a favourite with the Boundary Park faithful, especially when he scored 26 league and cup goals in the 1970/71 season; a major contributing factor to the Latics gaining promotion.

Fryatt's claim to fame is that he holds the record of the fastest-ever league goal, recorded at four seconds, which was scored for Bradford Park Avenue against Tranmere Rovers in 1964. A return of 42 goals in 79 starts was his record for Athletic before he moved back to old club Southport in 1971.

WEDNESDAY 3RD SEPTEMBER 1884

Athletic's first international player, George Woodger, was born in Croydon. He played for England in a 2-1 victory against Ireland on 11th February 1911. Nicknamed 'Lady', Woodger played 130 games for Athletic and scored 26 goals before signing for Tottenham Hotspur for £325 in 1914. George died in Croydon on 6th March 1961.

SATURDAY 4TH SEPTEMBER 1915

Athletic played their first wartime game, against Manchester United. The Latics won 3-2 and took gate receipts of £99 from a crowd of 4,420. Arthur Wolstenholme, Joe Walters and Arthur Gee got the Latics goals.

MONDAY 4TH SEPTEMBER 1939

Robert Mellor, the club secretary, made an announcement to the playing staff. Due to international tension and with World War II on the brink, all Boundary Park players had their contracts terminated. Other clubs were in the same boat.

SUNDAY 5TH SEPTEMBER 1880

Jimmy Hodson was born in Horwich and joined Athletic for a £15 fee when they were a Lancashire Combination outfit. He remained for ten years by which time the Latics were runners up in the First Division and went on to play in 289 games. He scored a solitary First Division goal, the winner against Sheffield Wednesday on 16th March 1912.

MONDAY 6TH SEPTEMBER 1943

David Best was born in Wareham, Dorset and made 98 Latics league appearances between 1966 and 1968. A very consistent goalkeeper, he was regarded as one of Athletic's best post-war custodians.

SATURDAY 6TH SEPTEMBER 1980

The Second Division home match against Sheffield Wednesday was held up for 29 minutes after the Wednesday fans started a riot. The incident that sparked the delay was the sending off of the Owls' Terry Curran for kicking Simon Stainrod. Wednesday fans invaded the pitch and many people left as the tension mounted. Parents could be seen taking their children away from Boundary Park as the Sheffield fans attacked the Chadderton Road end.

SATURDAY 6TH SEPTEMBER 2003

The Latics had the better chances in the game at Hartlepool United and managed to come away with a point after a hard-earned 0-0 draw. Their main concern was off the field. The club were in a position where they may not be able to complete their Division Two fixtures for the season after their recent financial troubles.

SATURDAY 7TH SEPTEMBER 1907

Athletic made their league debut in the Second Division at Stoke City. The game was billed as a mismatch, due to the fact that the Potters had spent most of their life in the First Division. Oldham had a good following out of the '12,000' watching and they were delighted when the visitors took the lead in the first half through Billy Dodds, the first ever league goal for the club. Watkins levelled for Stoke in the second half but goals from debutants Frank Newton and Jimmy Swarbrick gave the Latics a memorable 3-1 win in their inaugural game.

SATURDAY 7TH SEPTEMBER 1929

Scottish international and Boundary Park icon, Bobby Johnstone, was born in Selkirk. He was to have a huge impact on Athletic and he was to become the catalyst for a complete turnaround in fortunes for the club in the early 60s. One of the 'Famous Five' at Hibernian, he was to win one accolade after another in a distinguished career which took in a spell at Manchester City.

A gate of 17,116, the highest for six and a half years, flocked to see him make his debut at home to Exeter City and he put on a magnificent display. He was also a member of the team that beat Southport 11-0; he orchestrated the demolition on that day. Johnstone will always be fondly remembered by all who were honoured enough to see his creative skills on the field. He died in Selkirk on 22nd August 2001.

FRIDAY 7TH SEPTEMBER 1934

Former England schoolboy Jim Scott was born in Hetton-le-Hole. Signed from Burnley – where he was captain of their Central League team – he made 76 league appearances for Oldham. He was used mainly at left-half although he was versatile enough to be used on the right, and also at full-back.

TUESDAY 7TH SEPTEMBER 1948

Winger George McVitie was born in Carlisle. He was signed from West Bromwich Albion in 1972 for £20,000, a record fee for Oldham at the time. McVitie was a fast, direct player who excited the fans with some clever flank play. He scored 19 goals for the Latics in 113 league appearances before moving back to his hometown of Carlisle and was an ever-present in the championship winning team of 1973/74.

THURSDAY 8TH SEPTEMBER 1910

Freddie Worrall was born in Warrington. He signed for Athletic on amateur forms from Nantwich for £50 but a complicated transfer saga resulted in Bolton Wanderers being fined £50 for breaking league rules. The Latics got their man, but were fined £10. In all, Worrall appeared 107 times for Oldham, scoring 21 goals, before moving on to Portsmouth. He returned to Boundary Park in 1939 to play wartime football.

SATURDAY 8TH SEPTEMBER 1990

A lone goal by Ian Marshall at Barnsley was sufficient to keep Athletic on their promotion track. It was the Latics' fourth consecutive win and cemented their position as Second Division league leaders.

SATURDAY 8TH SEPTEMBER 2001

Oldham were lucky to beat Lancashire rivals Blackpool 2-1 in a home Division Two fixture. Darren Sheridan put the Latics ahead on the half hour mark. Brett Ormerod looked to have secured a point for the visitors but Lee Duxbury scored an 88th minute winner to send the majority of the 6,650 crowd wild. Manager Andy Ritchie made some odd tactical changes in what was a volatile game.

WEDNESDAY 9TH SEPTEMBER 1964

'Tricky' Ricky Holden was born in Skipton. He arrived at Boundary Park from Watford for £165,000 in 1989, just after Tommy Wright had been transferred to Leicester City for £100,000 less. He went on to become one of the greatest wingers to represent Athletic. A little on the tall side for a flank man, Holden could cross early, a ploy which Athletic took full advantage of in their glory times of the 'Pinch Me' years, and one which Roger Palmer exploited on many occasions. Holden was a major player in the promotion season which took Athletic back to the First Division after a break of 68 years. He was transferred to Manchester City in a deal worth £900,000 but later returned for a second spell but lost his place in the team when Graeme Sharp took over as manager from Joe Royle.

SATURDAY 10TH SEPTEMBER 1910

Newcastle United, FA Cup holders and powerhouse team of the First Division, provided the opposition for Athletic's first-ever home game in Division One. A record 34,000 excited fans filled Boundary Park to witness the event on a glorious day brimming with sunshine. The gate remained unbeaten until 1930. Unfortunately for the Latics fans, Newcastle won the game by a 2-0 score.

FRIDAY 10TH SEPTEMBER 1937

Walter Joyce was born in Oldham. Joyce had made a name for himself at neighbouring Burnley, then a leading First Division club, but he signed from Blackburn Rovers in 1967 and then became a member of the coaching staff for the 1969/70 season. He was a skilful player who gave great service to the club in his 71 league games. He scored just two goals.

FRIDAY 11TH SEPTEMBER 1936

Peter McCall was born in West Ham and played a major role in Athletic's promotion to Division Three. His debut came at home to Bradford City on 18th August 1962, a 2-1 Fourth Division win. A tall, but cool and casual wing-half, he played 108 league games and hit five goals in his three-year spell at Oldham.

TUESDAY 12th SEPTEMBER 2006

Athletic went to league leaders Nottingham Forest for a League One game. The Latics were in 18th place and pulled off a shock 2-0 win which silenced the Forest fans. In front of 17,446 supporters, Chris Porter hit a brace which convincingly shattered Forest's unbeaten home record in a game where Oldham completely outclassed the home side.

SATURDAY 13th SEPTEMBER 1941

Alan Lawson was born in Lennoxtown. Signed from Glasgow Celtic, Lawson served under five different managers in his six-year period at the club. On 28th August 1965 he became the first-ever substitute to appear for Athletic when he replaced Albert Jackson in the game against Peterborough United at Boundary Park. He scored his only goal for the club on that day even though he clocked up a total of 138 league appearances.

SATURDAY 14th SEPTEMBER 1957

The Latics played at Barrow in a Third Division (North) game and only one player was selected who had taken part in the previous outing, a 4-1 loss at Hartlepools United. Outside-right Ron Fawley was the lucky player to keep his place.

SATURDAY 14th SEPTEMBER 2002

Athletic ran riot over a ragged Mansfield Town in this Division Two game. Clyde Wijnhard hit four goals, Carlo Corazzin headed one in, and Wayne Andrews got his first goal for the club from the penalty spot. The Stags lost 6-1 and had conceded an amazing total of 28 goals in just eight games.

MONDAY 15th SEPTEMBER 1980

Football's top officials visited Boundary Park to investigate the riot from the game against Sheffield Wednesday on 6th September. Seven hours of talks were held and the FA Commission concluded that the ground and safety provisions were more than adequate and that the Owls should be held responsible for their fans' actions on that day. Athletic were totally exonerated from any blame.

SATURDAY 15TH SEPTEMBER 1990

Athletic continued their immaculate start to the Second Division campaign with their fifth consecutive league win, witnessed by 13,156 spectators. Oxford United were in the firing line for this Boundary Park encounter and goals from Ian Marshall, Earl Barrett and Neil Redfearn gave the Latics a resounding and convincing 3-0 victory. Marshall had hit six goals in the five matches and was proudly sitting on top of the leading goalscorers' list for the division.

MONDAY 16TH SEPTEMBER 1929

The Latics went to the top of the Second Division with a fine 3-2 win over Barnsley at Boundary Park. Bill Hasson grabbed two goals and Stewart Littlewood got the other in a match watched by 16,635 fans.

SATURDAY 16TH SEPTEMBER 1933

Athletic ran out 4-1 winners over West Ham United in the Second Division game played at Boundary Park. Watched by an 8,439 crowd, both teams were mid-table but the Hammers were never in the game as a force. The Latics marksmen on the day were Jack Pears, George Pateman, Arthur Bailey and Alf Agar.

TUESDAY 17TH SEPTEMBER 1968

Chairman Ken Bates resigned his position although he retained a seat on the board. He said, "The time has come when I have to concentrate more on my job than on football. After all, football has always been a hobby to me, an expensive hobby at that, and I have devoted more time and energy to it than a lot of people would have done". Within six months he had also resigned as a director of the club.

MONDAY 18TH SEPTEMBER 1893

Harry Grundy was born in Little Hulton and went on to play 289 games in 16 years with Athletic. He is best described, as follows, by a journalist of the time: "A fine back, who has done equally good service on either flank; a resolute, broad-shouldered clean player who has, all his days, been a credit to himself and his club."

EARL BARRETT SCORED IN SEPTEMBER 1990 AGAINST OXFORD. HERE HE IS AT THE END OF THE 1990/91 SEASON

SATURDAY 18TH SEPTEMBER 1948

Athletic lost 3-2 at home to Mansfield Town and had lost seven, and drawn one, of their first eight Third Division (North) matches. It was the worst start to a league season ever by any team in the Football League. Riddled with injuries, the introduction of Eric Gemmell was to be the catalyst for a change in fortunes for the club. His 23 league and cup goals, partnered with Ray Haddington's contribution, gave the striking partners a total of 45 goals for the season, a higher than average division total. The Latics finished the campaign in sixth place and just 10 points behind champions Hull City.

WEDNESDAY 18TH SEPTEMBER 1985

Matt Gray died in Oldham. A utility player who cost nothing more than a £10 signing-on fee when he came from Atherton, he gave great service to the club between 1928 and 1945. He scored 58 goals in 300 appearances and was rewarded with a benefit match against a Latics Old Boys XI in 1937.

SATURDAY 19TH SEPTEMBER 1936

Darlington was the venue for a fine 3-0 away win. 'Taffy' Jones, Norman Brunskill and Tommy Davis got the goals in a game that was watched by 6,195 spectators. The result left Athletic in sixth spot in the Third Division (North).

TUESDAY 19TH SEPTEMBER 1989

Athletic went to Leeds for a first leg League Cup game and came away with a 2-1 victory. Andy Ritchie and Rick Holden scored the goals. Who would have thought that it would be the springboard to send the Latics to the final at Wembley, their first ever visit?

SATURDAY 20TH SEPTEMBER 2003

A trip to the Causeway Stadium resulted in a remarkable away victory for the Latics, their fifth unbeaten game in Division Two. Wycombe Wanderers were 3-0 down at the halfway mark at their preferred stadium name of Adams Park with Paul Murray, Danny Hall and Calvin Zola getting the visitors' goals. A penalty from Chris Killen, and another effort from Murray, completed the 5-2 rout for the rampant Latics.

SATURDAY 21st SEPTEMBER 2002

A 1-0 win at Layer Road lifted Athletic to third in the Division Two table. A paltry 3,021 people showed up to watch a game where fortune smiled on the Latics. Clint Hill was sent off for serious foul play but a Wayne Andrews goal in the 64th minute was enough to settle the encounter.

TUESDAY 22nd SEPTEMBER 1970

Aldershot were the visitors to Boundary Park and the game turned out to be the best of the season, as Athletic put in a determined performance to beat them 5-2. Aldershot played their part in a game that was a credit to the Fourth Division as they matched the home side stride for stride. David Shaw led the goalscoring with a hat-trick and Jim Fryatt and Tommy Bryceland chipped in with a goal apiece.

WEDNESDAY 22nd SEPTEMBER 2004

Unbeaten Premiership side Tottenham Hotspur visited the Latics in a second round League Cup tie. Watched by 8,548 fans, Spurs were held at bay until the 37th minute when Frederic Kanoute put the visitors ahead. There was to be no giant-killing act, though, as the north Londoners went rampant in the second half, hitting another five goals, the last two coming in the last minute. The final score was 6-0, although the score flattered Spurs.

THURSDAY 23rd SEPTEMBER 1982

With 17% unemployment in the town and with dwindling gates, chairman Harry Wilde commissioned chartered accountants to help save the club. However, his attempts came to no avail and he handed in his resignation after eight years in the role, and 13 years as a director.

TUESDAY 24th SEPTEMBER 1912

Centre-forward Fred Howe was born in Bredbury and joined Athletic in 1946 when normal league football returned after the Second World War. His debut was against Carlisle United, a 2-0 home loss. He only played 31 games for Athletic but did find the net 20 times. His first goals came at Accrington Stanley – where he netted a brace, one a penalty – in the Latics' first win of the season and he followed it up with a hat-trick in the home 3-2 win against Rochdale.

TUESDAY 24th SEPTEMBER 1985

Athletic went to Anfield to take on Liverpool in the first leg of the League Cup second round. Having beaten Liverpool 1-0 in a pre-season friendly – the first game of player-manager Kenny Dalglish's reign – the Latics found the Reds a totally different proposition and went down 3-0, thus giving them a mountain to climb for the second leg.

TUESDAY 25th SEPTEMBER 1956

The Futcher twins were born in Chester. Paul was with Athletic from 1980 to 1983 and he won 11 under-21 caps for England. He established himself in defence and his cool and calm style made him an instant hit. He appeared in the league for the Latics 98 times, scoring once. His brother Ron was a clever centre-forward with a great first touch and he scored 30 goals in 65 league starts between 1985 and 1987.

MONDAY 26th SEPTEMBER 1949

Irish international Ronnie Blair was born in Coleraine. He notched up 405 appearances and scored 23 goals and 'scored' the 'goal' that was not given when Athletic beat Manchester United 1-0 in 1974. The strike beat United keeper Alex Stepney and rebounded from the angled stanchion in the goal and the referee waved play on, much to the amazement of the 26,356 spectators in the ground. Blair was brought back to Boundary Park for a second spell in 1972 from Rochdale by manager Jimmy Frizzell who negotiated a straight swap for Keith Bebbington. A testimonial game against an All-Ireland Select team in 1974 resulted in a 3-3 draw. Athletic's scorers were Paul Heaton, Vic Halom and Simon Stainrod.

THURSDAY 26th SEPTEMBER 1968

Ex-manager Jack Rowley returned for his second stint as manager of Athletic. Ken Bates had left the club and Rowley signed a two-year contract stating, "I am very pleased indeed to be back at Oldham. I realise, of course, that it will be a struggle, but it cannot be any worse than it has been". Having just left Bradford, Rowley had inherited a team at the bottom of the Third Division, with only one win in ten games and five goals scored and 23 against. He had a task on! Although improvement was made, it was not enough to avoid relegation as bottom club with just 35 points.

SATURDAY 27TH SEPTEMBER 1947

Oldham were searching for their first win of the Third Division (North) campaign after scoring only five goals in the first eight matches. They visited Darlington and could have been behind early on before Ray Haddington opened the scoring for the visitors. By the 58th minute Athletic had amazingly scored six goals, one more than their previous eight games put together! Haddington scored a hat-trick in front of the 7,296 supporters who turned up to watch the 6-0 hammering.

MONDAY 27TH SEPTEMBER 1948

Les Chapman was born at Boundary Park Hospital, Oldham and, after playing for Chadderton Boys, went to Huddersfield Town as an amateur. He joined Athletic as a trialist and turned professional in January 1967 before going back to Leeds Road in exchange for David Shaw. Chapman had a second spell at Boundary Park in 1974/75 when he was involved in a deal that took Colin Garwood to Leeds Road. He performed well but he was surprisingly released on a free transfer to Stockport County. Chapman made 289 appearances for the Latics with a return of 23 goals.

THURSDAY 28TH SEPTEMBER 1950

Manager Billy Wootton resigned after the Latics had lost six of their opening eight games in the Third Division (North). His resignation coincided with a change of chairman as Mr Herbert Gartside JP took over from Mr Percy Skipworth. Mr Gartside announced to the press, "I have nothing to add," whereas Mr Wootton was quoted as saying, "not a word".

SATURDAY 28TH SEPTEMBER 2002

This Division Two 'Roses Battle' turned out to be a one-sided affair as former boss Mick Wadsworth brought his Huddersfield Town team to Boundary Park. Current manager Iain Dowie certainly pulled one over on his mentor as Athletic swept aside the Terriers by a convincing 4-0 scoreline. Clyde Wijnhard got two goals and David Eyres and Lourenco completed the scoring. It was Athletic's fifth successive win.

SATURDAY 29TH SEPTEMBER 1990

Athletic forced a 0-0 draw at West Bromwich Albion to retain top spot in Division Two but they were fined by the Football League for showing up late for the match.

SATURDAY 30TH SEPTEMBER 1933

A struggling Manchester United travelled up the road to take on Athletic in a Second Division game but travelled back home empty handed after a 2-0 defeat. Jack Pears got both the goals in front of a healthy 22,736 gate.

SATURDAY 30TH SEPTEMBER 1950

High-flying Tranmere Rovers went away from Boundary Park with the points after a thrilling 4-3 game watched by over 13,000 spectators. Ray Haddington got two goals and Jimmy Munro added another, but it was not enough and the Rovers finished the day in second spot in the Third Division (North), just behind Gateshead on goal difference.

TUESDAY 30TH SEPTEMBER 2003

Over 7,000 people were present at Boundary Park when local neighbours Stockport County visited for a Division Two game. John Sheridan scored a penalty after Calvin Zola was brought down. Scott Vernon killed off the game when he fired home a Chris Killen rebound. It was Athletic's third successive win and gave some hope of encouraging a potential investor to help the cash-strapped team.

OLDHAM ATHLETIC
On This Day

OCTOBER

SATURDAY 1st OCTOBER 1960

Ken Branagan made his Athletic debut against York City in front of 9,284 expectant supporters in this Fourth Division fixture. A penalty from Peter Phoenix and goals from Brian Birch and Bert Lister gave the home side a 3-1 victory.

THURSDAY 1st OCTOBER 1964

Midfield maestro John Sheridan was born in Stretford. He joined Athletic in July 2001 from Doncaster Rovers to join up with his old pal and ex-Leeds United colleague Andy Ritchie. An Irish international, Sheridan featured in two World Cup squads; Italia '90 and USA '94. In his first season, his creative play helped the Latics avoid relegation and he was voted the supporters' 'Player of the Year'. In October 2001, manager Ritchie was sacked and was succeeded by Mick Wadsworth then, in May 2002, head coach Iain Dowie was appointed as the new boss with Sheridan promoted to a player/coaching role.

When Dowie resigned, with the club in turmoil over the Chris Moore fiasco, Sheridan took over as acting manager and was assisted by David Eyres. The managerial merry-go-round continued and Sheridan then took a role as assistant to Brian Talbot. A successful spell as reserve team manager resulted in Sheridan eventually taking full control as manager on 1st June 2006 when he replaced the outgoing Ronnie Moore. Sheridan made 164 appearances and scored 16 goals for Athletic.

SATURDAY 2nd OCTOBER 1920

Les Smith was born in Manchester. He joined Athletic as a part-time professional in July 1949. Under Billy Wootton, Smith was tried in several positions but an injury left him out of favour. When George Hardwick took over, he was given a new lease of life and went on to play 192 games for the Latics, with four goals to his credit. He was also part of the team to win the Third Division (North) championship. Les died in Hazel Grove on 6th December 2001.

TUESDAY 2ND OCTOBER 1990

Fellow promotion contenders Swindon Town visited Oldham and put on a great show that probably deserved more than returning home with nothing. Athletic eked out a 3-2 win with goals from Paul Moulden, Rick Holden and a late penalty from Neil Redfearn. The win, witnessed by 12,575, saw the Latics maintain their unbeaten league form.

WEDNESDAY 2ND OCTOBER 2002

A second round League Cup game was played at Pride Park. Over 1,500 hardy Athletic fans made the trip to watch their heroes, who had only tasted defeat twice in this season. Derby took the lead in the 17th minute but David Eyres levelled the scores just sixty seconds later and that's how it stayed until full-time. The Latics got a penalty awarded in extra time. Clyde Wijnhard stepped up to easily convert the spot kick to give the Latics a deserved 2-1 victory and safe passage into the third round.

SUNDAY 3RD OCTOBER 1948

Ex-Sunderland FA Cup winner Vic Halom was born in Burton-upon-Trent. Known as the 'King of all Geordies' to the Latics faithful, Halom was an uncompromising centre-forward with a good eye for goal. He was the club's leading goalscorer with 19 goals in his first season at Oldham and in all, scored 43 times in 123 league games.

MONDAY 3RD OCTOBER 1955

Ged Keegan was born in Little Hulton. He signed from Manchester City after helping the Maine Road outfit win the League Cup in 1976. He was inspirational in helping the club move away from the lower reaches of the league table. Ginger-haired Keegan got five goals in 144 league games for the Latics.

TUESDAY 3RD OCTOBER 1961

Local First Division side Burnley brought their star-studded team to Boundary Park for a friendly game to inaugurate the switching on of the new floodlights. The Oldham public helped to raise some of the £18,000 required.

TUESDAY 3RD OCTOBER 1989

Leeds United came to Boundary Park for a second-leg League Cup game. Athletic dispensed with them 2-1 and went through 4-2 on aggregate. Frankie Bunn and Andy Ritchie got the goals to set up a meeting with Scarborough in the next round, a game which was to become a record-breaker.

TUESDAY 4TH OCTOBER 1939

Arguably one of the best goalscorers ever to put on an Oldham shirt, Bert Lister was born in Miles Platting. Manager Jack Rowley paid £10,000 to bring him from Manchester City in a double deal with Ken Branagan. As a centre-forward, he would have gone through a brick wall to score with one of his brilliant diving headers. In 1963 he almost broke the all-time record for goals in a season and his six goals against Southport on Boxing Day 1962 will always be remembered.

His success began when he teamed up with Bobby Johnstone. Bert later played for Rochdale and finished his playing career at Stockport County. He achieved a remarkable 97 goals in 153 games for the Latics and had the distinction of scoring against Chesterfield in 1963 within 10 seconds of the kick-off. It was a sad loss when he died of a heart attack in 2007.

TUESDAY 5TH OCTOBER 1937

Big Bob Ledger was born in Craghead, County Durham. The 6ft 1ins player signed for Athletic in 1962 from Huddersfield Town for a fee of £6,000 and went on to make 240 appearances for the club. A versatile player who played in nearly every position for the Latics, he was a great crosser of the ball. He scored on his debut in a 2-1 win at Bradford City on 18th August 1962 and was an ever-present member of the 1962/63 Third Division promotion-winning team. Ledger scored a total of 38 goals in his five years at Boundary Park.

FRIDAY 5TH OCTOBER 1951

Scottish international Willie Donachie was born in Castlemilk, Glasgow. Donachie made his name at Manchester City and the evergreen player was appointed player/coach for Athletic in 1985. Originally a midfielder, he was equally at home at full-back and went on to become Joe Royle's right-hand man in the Latics successful team that reached the FA Cup semi-finals twice and the League Cup final. He won a total of 35 caps and played for Scotland in the 1978 World Cup finals. He played 190 games for Athletic and got three goals before he reluctantly retired from playing at the age of 42.

SATURDAY 5TH OCTOBER 2002

The 1-0 win at Swindon Town was achieved with a low shot from Lee Duxbury. It was the eighth consecutive win for a Latics team who were on a roll, and it cemented their position as league leaders in Division Two.

SATURDAY 6TH OCTOBER 1923

Athletic entertained Manchester United in the Second Division at Boundary Park in front of 15,120 supporters. The match marked the debut of Frank Hargreaves. It was a remarkable game in which Sammy Wynne gave the visitors the lead through an own goal but he then made amends with a penalty conversion on the half-hour mark. Ten minutes into the second half, Billy Howson put Athletic ahead and on the hour mark Wynne scored again to make it 3-1. However, Wynne amazingly scored another own goal to become the only player to score two goals at each end in one match. The final score was 3-2 to Athletic.

WEDNESDAY 6TH OCTOBER 1965

Hull City welcomed Athletic to Boothferry Park for a Third Division game, but the courtesies ended there as they went on to consolidate their promotion bid by hammering the Latics 5-1. Over 17,000, the highest gate in the division, saw the demolition. Albert Jackson got the only goal for the visitors who remained second bottom.

SATURDAY 6TH OCTOBER 1990

Blackburn Rovers brought their team to Oldham to see if they could inflict the first defeat of the season on the runaway Second Division league leaders. A Paul Moulden goal, on a windswept day at Boundary Park, looked to have clinched another victory for the rampant Latics but the Rovers won a share of the points with a last-gasp effort in the dying seconds of the contest. It was only Moulden's second goal since signing from AFC Bournemouth in March for a fee of £225,000.

TUESDAY 7TH OCTOBER 1947

Local lad Paul Edwards was born in Shaw. The England under-23 international started 112 league games for the Latics and scored seven goals. He was a versatile defender and helped them win seven and draw one from his first eleven games for the club.

TUESDAY 7TH OCTOBER 1969

Latics captain Lee Duxbury was born at Skipton. A tenacious midfielder, he had the knack of scoring important goals. Neil Warnock signed him from Bradford City in 1997 but poor performances resulted in Athletic being relegated from Division One. When Iain Dowie took over as manager he demoted him and gave the captaincy to Matty Appleby, telling Duxbury that he was free to leave. When Chris Moore started to sell off the Latics players, Duxbury reluctantly signed for neighbours Bury, after admitting that he hadn't been paid for six weeks. He made 278 appearances and scored 38 goals for Athletic. When John Sheridan was appointed the Latics boss in 2006, Duxbury was recruited and returned to Boundary Park as reserve team manager.

SATURDAY 8TH OCTOBER 1938

A trip to Valley Parade brought huge rewards with a finely executed win over Bradford City in front of more than 6,000 fans. Ernest Wright, David Halford and Jack Diamond (2) got the goals which left Athletic in third place in the Third Division (North) table.

SATURDAY 8TH OCTOBER 1977

Tottenham Hotspur gave the Latics a finishing lesson when they ran out 5-1 victors at White Hart Lane in this Second Division game. Alan Young got the only Latics goal in a match watched by 24,636 fans.

WEDNESDAY 8TH OCTOBER 1986

Elland Road was buzzing with 11,449 fans anticipating that Leeds would overcome a 3-2 deficit in the second leg of the second round of the League Cup. Two goals from Ron Futcher and one from Andy Linighan had given the Latics a first leg lead. On the night, it took a lone goal from ace poacher Roger Palmer to secure a great 1-0 away victory for the Latics, sending them through with a 4-2 aggregate score.

SATURDAY 9TH OCTOBER 1909

Boundary Park was chosen to stage a game between the Football League and their Irish League counterparts. Latics keeper Howard Mathews played in goal for the League, and was probably the best uncapped goalkeeper at the time. The League side won the contest 9-1.

WEDNESDAY 9TH OCTOBER 1985

Athletic entertained Liverpool in a second leg League Cup game. Starting three goals down from the first leg it would be a tough test. The Latics were given a lesson by their opponents, going down 5-2 and thus losing 8-2 on aggregate. Ironically, Liverpool old boy and 'super-sub' David Fairclough got both of Athletic's goals against his old club.

FRIDAY 9TH OCTOBER 1987

Scotland's goalkeeper Andy Goram was transferred to Hibernian for a fee of £325,000. He had made 192 league starts for Oldham and had established himself as an extremely capable keeper.

WEDNESDAY 10TH OCTOBER 1962

Mark Ward was born in Huyton. He scored 12 goals in 84 league games before being surprisingly snapped up by West Ham for £250,000. The fee was a remarkable return on a player who had been signed from Northwich Victoria for a fee of just £10,000.

SATURDAY 11TH OCTOBER 1941

Jim Bowie was born in Howwood, Renfrewshire. Bowie was signed from Arthurlie Juniors and the tall inside-forward/half back went on to notch up 365 appearances for Athletic while hitting 42 goals in the process.

MONDAY 11TH OCTOBER 1948

Crowd-pleaser David Shaw was born in Huddersfield. In his two spells at Oldham, Shaw hit 95 goals in 229 games. He will be remembered for his blistering pace and he certainly knew where the net was! He formed a lethal partnership with big Jim Fryatt and their contribution in the 1970/71 season was a major one which helped Athletic almost monopolise the Ford Sporting League. The club earned £70,000 from the competition which built a new stand at the Broadway side of the ground. Shaw was transferred to West Bromwich Albion in an £80,000 move but he was forced to retire in 1978 after a troublesome knee injury.

WEDNESDAY 11TH OCTOBER 1950

Quick-thinking Ian Towers was born at Blackhill. He made his debut with three other new faces in the Third Division (North) home match with Shrewsbury Town in January 1966. He was a team-mate of former player-manager Jimmy McIlroy who gave a good return of 45 goals in 95 league outings for the Latics in the mid sixties.

SATURDAY 12TH OCTOBER 1985

The Latics went to Crystal Palace but goals from Roger Palmer and David Fairclough were not enough as they went down 3-2. Having lost just two of their first 10 games, Athletic were still in third place in the Second Division.

SATURDAY 13TH OCTOBER 1990

A trip to Boothferry Park to take on Hull City resulted in Athletic maintaining their unbeaten Second Division league run but it wasn't without a scare. The Latics were two goals down just after half-time but they fought back to earn a point with goals from Nick Henry and Neil Redfearn in front of 8,676 supporters.

LATICS LEGEND ROGER PALMER WAS ON TARGET AT CRYSTAL PALACE IN OCTOBER 1985

SATURDAY 14th OCTOBER 2000

Latics legend David Eyres made his Division Two debut for Athletic. A crowd of 4,009 gathered to watch the Blues beat Swindon Town 1-0 at Boundary Park.

WEDNESDAY 15th OCTOBER 1902

Ted Goodier was born in Little Hulton. He joined Athletic from Lancaster Town in 1925 and went on to get three goals in 116 appearances. In 1931 he moved to Queens Park Rangers but returned to the club as manager in 1956. He showed good business sense in the transfer market spending only £900 in his two years in charge, but raking in £39,000 from player sales. In his first season as boss he used no fewer than 31 players, of which 19 were new signings.

SATURDAY 15th OCTOBER 1960

Cult hero Bobby Johnstone played his first game for Athletic against Exeter City at Boundary Park to kick-start an era that will be forever remembered in the history of Oldham Athletic. He signed for £4,000 from Manchester City – surely one of the best ever deals by the club. The Latics were rock bottom of the Fourth Division but Johnstone put in a remarkable performance which enthralled the 17,116 success-starved Oldham fans. He mesmerised the crowd with his deft touches and subtle tricks and his virtuoso performance – including a debut goal – helped Athletic to a convincing 5-2 victory. A new era had begun at Oldham.

SUNDAY 16th OCTOBER 1960

Scottish international striker Graeme Sharp was born in Glasgow. Joe Royle brought him to Athletic from Everton for a fee of £500,000 in 1991 and he was to make 134 appearances, scoring 36 goals, for the Latics. He was appointed player-manager to replace Royle, who had taken on the manager's job at Everton. With Athletic struggling at the wrong end of the First Division, Sharp was released from his duties in 1997 to be succeeded by Neil Warnock.

SATURDAY 17TH OCTOBER 1908

Latics legend and flying winger Joe Donnachie made his Second Division debut in the home match against Birmingham City when goals from William Andrews and Arthur Wolstenholme gave Oldham a 2-0 win. Donnachie also played in the Athletic team that made its debut in the First Division. In total, he played in 238 games and, as more of a provider than scorer, he managed to net on 21 occasions.

SATURDAY 18TH OCTOBER 1913

An estimated crowd of 20,000 piled into Boundary Park to watch the Latics take on Newcastle United in a First Division game. Oliver Tummon, Arthur Gee and Joe Walters got the goals which hoisted the Latics up to fourth spot in the league table.

SATURDAY 18TH OCTOBER 1924

A Second Division relegation battle ensued as South Shields came to town. The Latics ran out 1-0 victors with a goal from Jack Keedwell but both teams avoided being demoted at the end of the season.

SATURDAY 18TH OCTOBER 1930

The Latics beat Second Division strugglers Cardiff City 4-2 at home. Jimmy Dyson (2), Fred Worrall and Stewart Littlewood got the goals.

SATURDAY 18TH OCTOBER 1980

Promotion-chasing West Ham United earned a 0-0 draw in a Second Division match at Boundary Park. The Hammers were left in second spot, one point behind Notts County at the end of the day.

SATURDAY 19TH OCTOBER 1907

A 2-1 win at Fulham was enough to leave Athletic sitting fifth in the Second Division. Billy Dodds and Frank Newton got the all important goals. Leicester Fosse, Gainsborough Trinity, Glossop North End and Clapton Orient were all members of the Second Division at the time.

SATURDAY 19TH OCTOBER 1935

The Latics beat their closest neighbours Rochdale at Spotland, 6-2, in this Third Division (North) fixture. Norman Brunskill, Alf Agar, Fred Leedham (2) and Arthur Buckley (2) did the damage.

TUESDAY 19th OCTOBER 1965

Bristol Rovers hammered Athletic 4-0 in a Third Division fixture. The result left Athletic bottom having secured just six points from 13 games.

TUESDAY 19th OCTOBER 2004

The visit of Bristol City resulted in a 0-0 scoreline and increased Athletic's dismal run to seven games without a victory in League One. Considering that Jermain Johnson was sent off with fifteen minutes remaining, manager Brian Talbot was satisfied with the result.

TUESDAY 20th OCTOBER 1981

Second Division Oldham went to Charlton Athletic and lost 3-1. It was the team's first loss of the season, the last one in the entire Football League. Jim Steel got the only Latics goal on the day.

SATURDAY 21st OCTOBER 1911

West Bromwich Albion visited Boundary Park for a First Division game and left reeling from a 3-1 defeat. Evan Jones got two goals and Tom Marrison bagged one in front of around 15,000 fans.

SATURDAY 21st OCTOBER 1961

Struggling Fourth Division Oldham went to Gresty Road and came away victorious after a thrilling 5-3 victory over Crewe Alexandra. Bert Lister and Johnny Colquhoun both got two goals and Jimmy Frizzell also scored in a game watched by 6,504 fans.

SATURDAY 22nd OCTOBER 2005

A thrilling 4-3 win over Bristol City was Athletic's first win in six. A poor crowd of 5,456 watched Mark Hughes, Ritchie Wellens, Chris Porter and Andy Liddell strike to leave Athletic in 10th place in League One.

FRIDAY 23rd OCTOBER 1925

Frank Tomlinson was born in Manchester. He signed from Goslings FC – where he had already hit 23 goals in less than three months – on 16th November 1946. Tomlinson enjoyed success as a speedy winger with a quick and deceptive turn of pace and in the 1948/49 campaign he was third leading goalscorer. He scored 29 goals in a total of 124 games for the Latics and passed away in Oldham on 20th April 1999.

SATURDAY 23RD OCTOBER 1954

The Latics drew 2-2 at Gateshead. Kenny Chaytor made his Athletic debut at the age of 16 years and 11 months. Known as the 'Durham wonderkid', he became one of the youngest players ever to represent the club. The result left Oldham in 18th place with 13 points in the Third Division (North), while the Tynesiders sat sixth with 20.

SUNDAY 24TH OCTOBER 1948

Alan Groves was born in Ainsdale, Southport. He was a firm crowd favourite at Boundary Park and was signed by Jimmy Frizzell from AFC Bournemouth for £10,000 in 1973. The football world was shocked when he died from a massive heart attack at the tender age of 29.

SUNDAY 25TH OCTOBER 1931

Athletic manager Jimmy McIlroy was born in Lembeg, near Lisburn. The Irish international, who made his name with Burnley, became Latics manager in 1966 when chairman Ken Bates appointed him to take charge of the-then bottom team of the Third Division. A player crisis forced him to return to playing just short of his 36th birthday and he went on the make 39 league appearances, scoring just one goal.

SATURDAY 25TH OCTOBER 1959

Alan McNeill made his Athletic debut at home to Aldershot. The Latics were on a poor run which was reflected by the paltry 3,275 spectators who bothered to show up for this Fourth Division fixture. The home side were soon two goals down, but McNeill scored on his debut and Jim Bowie levelled the scores. In the second half John Bingham, and another goal from Bowie, gave the Latics a 4-2 win.

WEDNESDAY 25TH OCTOBER 1989

Athletic recorded their biggest ever League Cup win when they beat Scarborough 7-0. Frankie Bunn got six goals on the night and at one stage the scoreboard read Bunn 6 Scarborough 0! First Division champions Arsenal was the reward for the Latics in the next round.

WEDNESDAY 26TH OCTOBER 1955

Kirkcaldy was the birthplace of Alan Young. The big centre-forward scored 30 times in 122 league appearances in his five-year stay at Oldham. He scored a hat-trick against Leicester City in the fourth round of the FA Cup in 1979, a feat that encouraged Leicester to splash out a fee of £250,000 to take him to Filbert Street in the same year.

TUESDAY 26TH OCTOBER 1965

Goalkeeper Jon Hallworth was born in Hazel Grove. He signed from Ipswich Town to join a struggling team fighting against relegation. Hallworth replaced Andy Rhodes who was dropped after conceding four goals at Barnsley. He had an immediate impact on a team that had not won in 15 games, helping Athletic to an unbeaten run of ten games. He went on to make 214 appearances before being transferred to Cardiff City in 1997 but he was to return to the Latics as part-time goalkeeping coach in 2001.

TUESDAY 27TH OCTOBER 1914

Jack Hurst was born in Lever Bridge near Bolton. Jack was almost a veteran when he joined Athletic from Bolton Wanderers in 1947 for a fee of £1,510. New manager Billy Wootton waited until mid-season before he gave Hurst his debut and he went on to score two goals in 107 games. He left the club in 1950/51 when he joined Chelmsford City.

THURSDAY 27TH OCTOBER 1988

Paul Warhurst was snapped up for £10,000 from Manchester City. He amassed a total of 86 games before he was transferred to Sheffield Wednesday for £750,000. Warhurst would go on to play for a further 17 clubs, including Blackburn Rovers and Bolton Wanderers.

SATURDAY 27TH OCTOBER 1990

A 2-1 win over Notts County completed three consecutive victories and helped to consolidate the Latics' position as top dogs in the Second Division as well as maintaining their still-unbeaten league record. Neil Redfearn and Andy Ritchie supplied the goals which were acknowledged by 12,940 enthusiastic supporters.

SATURDAY 28TH OCTOBER 1933

An enthralling Second Division game ensued at Boundary Park as two bottom-half teams met in a Lancashire versus Yorkshire clash. Visitors Bradford City ran out losers in a seven-goal thriller. Arthur Bailey, Tommy Reid (2) and 'pocket Hercules' Cliff Chadwick netted for the Latics' goals.

SATURDAY 28TH OCTOBER 1995

Athletic went down 2-1 at Derby County. Pushing for a play-off spot in the First Division, Sean McCarthy got the only goal of the game for Oldham.

SATURDAY 28TH OCTOBER 2006

This League One game resulted in a 3-1 win for the Latics over struggling Brentford. In a match watched by less than 5,000 spectators, Oldham stretched their unbeaten home run to seven matches while the Bees registered their tenth game without a win. Goals by Paul Warne, Gary McDonald and Richie Wellens sealed the victory.

TUESDAY 29TH OCTOBER 1935

Royton was the birthplace of Bolton Wanderers' great goalkeeper Eddie Hopkinson. He achieved a remarkable total of 519 league and 59 FA Cup games for the Wanderers in an 18-year career at Burnden Park. After playing for local side Haggate Lads he made just three appearances as an amateur for the Latics before he moved to Burnden Park. It is generally accepted that Hopkinson was the youngest ever player to make his debut when he played for Athletic at an age of 16 years and 75 days.

TUESDAY 29TH OCTOBER 1957

Gary Hoolickin was born in Middleton and joined Athletic as a 16-year-old. 'Mr Versatile' clocked up 241 appearances and three goals in his twelve years at Boundary Park, but it was his misfortune to be an understudy to the ever-reliable Ian Wood. Hoolickin's career virtually ended in a pre-season friendly in 1987 when he injured his knee and had to accept the specialists' advice that he was finished. He was granted a testimonial game against Manchester City in 1986.

TUESDAY 29TH OCTOBER 2002

The 4-0 win over Northampton Town kept Athletic on track for promotion from Division Two. They finished the game one point behind league leaders Cardiff City. Goals from Wayne Andrews, Carlo Corazzin, David Eyres and John Eyre did enough but even though the score was convincing, the Cobblers could feel hard done by on the night.

SATURDAY 30TH OCTOBER 1926

Athletic played Southampton and a goal by Albert Pynegar gave the Latics a point in a 1-1 draw. Making his debut in the game – watched by 17,881 fans – was goalkeeper Jack Hacking. Oldham occupied eighth spot in the Second Division after the result.

TUESDAY 30TH OCTOBER 2007

The Latics dragged themselves out of the League One relegation zone with a fine 0-0 draw at Nottingham Forest in front of 16,423 supporters at the City Ground. Athletic had the better of the play on the night and spurned enough chances to have won against a Forest side who were sitting comfortably in a play-off spot.

SUNDAY 31ST OCTOBER 1965

Denis Irwin was born in Cork. Signed on a free transfer from Leeds United, Irwin went on to establish himself as one of the best full-backs outside the First Division. He appeared in 199 Oldham games and scored seven goals, most of them rockets from free-kicks. He was transferred to Manchester United in 1990 for £625,000 – Athletic's record incoming fee – after giving consistently good service and missing few games. He went on to give 12 years of consistent displays for Manchester United before being given a free transfer to Wolverhampton Wanderers, where he ended his career.

OLDHAM ATHLETIC
On This Day

NOVEMBER

SATURDAY 1st NOVEMBER 1919

The Latics beat Derby County by a convincing 3-0 margin in this First Division fixture. A total of 8,893 fans watched George Wall, Bill Bradbury and Arthur Wolstenhulme score the goals that saw off the Rams.

SATURDAY 1st NOVEMBER 1952

Southport came to Boundary Park and were on the receiving end of a 3-0 walloping. The win left the Latics in second place in the Third Division (North), just one point behind leaders Grimsby Town. In a match watched by over 17,000 people the goals were scored by Jimmy Munro, Peter McKennan and Eric Gemmell.

SATURDAY 1st NOVEMBER 2003

Plymouth Argyle dropped their first points for five matches in a 2-2 draw at Home Park. In an ill-tempered match the Latics had John Sheridan and Paul Murray sent off while the Pilgrims also had a player red carded for violent conduct. David Beharall scored both Athletic goals in a Division Two game which entertained over 11,000 spectators.

THURSDAY 2nd NOVEMBER 1967

Steve Redmond was born in Liverpool. He arrived at Oldham in July 1992 to join Joe Royle's team for their first season back in the First Division after many years in the lower-league wilderness. As Latics favourite Rick Holden made the move to Manchester City, Royle brought Redmond and Neil Pointon in the opposite direction, plus a cash payment. In July 1998, Redmond was granted a free transfer to Bury after playing in 237 games for Athletic and scoring five goals.

SATURDAY 2nd NOVEMBER 1985

Athletic lost 1-0 at Barnsley. Having lost just three of their first 14 games the Latics had been in second spot in the Second Division. The loss severely knocked their confidence and it began a run of ten losses in 11 games, the other result being a draw. Athletic dropped like a stone and they ended up fifth from bottom after their dreadful run.

SATURDAY 2ND NOVEMBER 2002

Teenager Scott Vernon made his debut in the clash against local rivals Stockport County in Division Two. Over 8,000 fans were at Boundary Park as Fitz Hall nodded in from close range to put the Blues ahead in the 40th minute. The clincher came in the last minute when debutant Vernon slid the ball home from 10 yards to send the home crowd wild.

WEDNESDAY 3RD NOVEMBER 1965

Bill Walsh died in his home town of Blackpool. He was a prolific goalscorer and was the leading marksman in the Third Division (North) with 32 goals in the 1935/36 season. His total record for Athletic was 48 goals in 77 league games.

SATURDAY 3RD NOVEMBER 1990

The biggest gate to attend any Second Division game all season assembled at Hillsborough to watch Sheffield Wednesday entertain Athletic. In one of the most entertaining games of the campaign, the 34,845 in attendance witnessed a feast of football which ended in a 2-2 draw. Tony Henry and David Currie got the goals for Athletic. The game was the Latics 15th unbeaten game since the beginning of the season, a record that bettered their previous best of 13, which went back to 1953.

TUESDAY 4TH NOVEMBER 1930

Ted West was born in Parbold, Lancashire. West was a steady and reliable full-back who played in 117 league games for Oldham. Upon leaving the Latics in 1961 he went to play in Australia.

SATURDAY 5TH NOVEMBER 1921

Championship-chasing Sunderland hammered Athletic 5-1 in a First Division match witnessed by around 25,000 buoyant fans. Reuben Butler got the only Oldham goal on the day.

SATURDAY 5TH NOVEMBER 1960

Athletic travelled to non-league Rhyl for a first round FA Cup game which was seen by approximately 7,000 fans. Bert Lister scored the only goal of the game which put the Latics through to the next round, an away tie at Chesterfield.

TUESDAY 5TH NOVEMBER 1968

Bottom of the Third Division, Athletic sprung a surprise result with a 1-0 win at Shrewsbury Town. David 'Dickie' Down notched the only goal of the game. It was Down's solitary strike for Athletic who were relegated at the end of the season.

TUESDAY 6TH NOVEMBER 1962

Athletic's goalscoring hero Frankie Bunn was born in Birmingham. Signed from Hull City for £90,000, he helped to transform a poor scoring side into one of the most lethal scoring machines ever seen at Boundary Park. Bunn played a total of 88 games for the Latics, scoring 35 goals in his three seasons at Oldham.

He scored six goals in a League Cup game against Scarborough and played his final game for Athletic in the League Cup final against Nottingham Forest at Wembley. Bunn was replaced by Roger Palmer after 67 minutes with a knee injury which was to prove too hard to fight back from. Surgery and a 19-month fight for fitness ended with Bunn having to retire from the game. It was a sad day for all at Boundary Park.

WEDNESDAY 6TH NOVEMBER 2002

A trip to West Ham United in the third round of the League Cup was the daunting task for promotion-chasing Athletic and almost 22,000 supporters were there to witness the game. The Hammers had a lot of the possession but the Latics shook the home team minutes from the half-time whistle when Carlo Corazzin powered home a header from a David Eyres corner. Try as they may, the Hammers just couldn't get the final touch to do any reciprocal damage.

This game had everything; end-to-end play, great saves and even a West Ham streaker. The home side threw everything at Oldham, all to no avail. The final whistle cued amazing scenes of jubilation for the 951 travelling Athletic fans.

SUNDAY 6TH NOVEMBER 2005

A capacity crowd of 1,997, with millions more watching live on worldwide TV, crammed into the Scholars Ground to see if little Chasetown could cause the biggest upset in the history of the FA Cup. Chasetown had never played league opposition before and the Staffordshire team were seven leagues and 133 places below Athletic in the pyramid. Chasetown took the lead after an own goal by goalkeeper Chris Day but David Eyres stepped up to save the visitors' blushes with a cracking equaliser in the 31st minute. Chasetown had earned a money-spinning replay...

TUESDAY 6TH NOVEMBER 2007

The short trip to Prenton Park to take on Tranmere Rovers resulted in a 1-0 win for Athletic. A 90th minute goal from Craig Davies sealed the points in front of 5,473 supporters. Not many of the Latics fans who travelled on the night would have believed that the win would be the start of a record-breaking nine League One away games without defeat.

WEDNESDAY 7TH NOVEMBER 1962

Darron McDonough was born in Antwerp, Belgium. He scored on his Fourth Division debut for Athletic at Notts County in 1980 as a young 18-year-old and totalled 200 appearances, netting 17 times. He always gave 100% and was used as a striker, midfielder and defender in his nine-year spell at Boundary Park. He left the club under a cloud of smoke after a contractual disagreement, much to the dismay of the supporters.

SATURDAY 8TH NOVEMBER 2003

A goal by Calvin Zola and two from Ernie Cooksey were sufficient to see off any challenge that Carlisle United might have offered in this first-round FA Cup match at Boundary Park, watched by 4,391 fans.

SATURDAY 9TH NOVEMBER 1929

The Latics were in second place in the Second Division and they sent Wolverhampton Wanderers home with their tails between their legs after dishing out a 6-0 thrashing to their championship challengers.

SATURDAY 9th NOVEMBER 2002

A David Eyres penalty and a Wayne Andrews volley in a two-minute spell of the second half of this Division Two game gave Athletic a share of the points in an enthralling game at Plymouth Argyle. The Pilgrims were two goals up within the first seven minutes but the draw was enough for the Latics to sit at the top of the league table again.

SATURDAY 10th NOVEMBER 1923

A 2-0 loss at South Shields left Athletic floundering in 17th place in the Second Division table while South Shield hoisted themselves into second place just one point behind league leaders Leeds United.

SATURDAY 10th NOVEMBER 1928

Ashton Gate was the venue for a bottom-of-the-table Second Division clash between Bristol City and Athletic. The result of the meeting was a terrible 6-0 mauling that left the Latics one off the bottom of the league with a measly six points from 14 games. City were not much better off, being a place higher with just two points more.

SATURDAY 10th NOVEMBER 1973

Hereford United were the visitors for a thrilling game of Third Division football at Boundary Park. United played their part in an enthralling 4-3 win for the home side, and were unlucky to leave empty handed. The result left the Latics in second place and still on course for promotion. George Jones got two goals, and Andy Lochhead and Ronnie Blair chipped in with the others.

THURSDAY 10th NOVEMBER 1994

Everton had sacked manager Mike Walker just two days ago and all the speculation about Athletic's manager Joe Royle finally came to fruition when he joined the Toffees as their new boss. Oldham had been struggling in a less-than-impressive start to the season and the Latics faithful finally had to accept that their most successful manager ever was on his way out of Boundary Park.

SATURDAY 10TH NOVEMBER 2007

Doncaster Rovers visited the Latics for an FA Cup game before a miserable crowd of just over 4,000. Neil Trotman's first goal of the season put Athletic ahead and Craig Davies made it 2-0 but James Hayter hit a double for the Rovers to earn them a replay.

SATURDAY 11TH NOVEMBER 1950

The Third Division (North) home game against Lincoln City had an unusually large attendance of 21,742, with many coming to watch the debut of former England star George Hardwick. The game was a 0-0 draw but it marked the beginning of a new and exciting era at Boundary Park.

TUESDAY 11TH NOVEMBER 1980

Jim Steel scored the only goal of the Second Division match at Boundary Park which saw off neighbours Blackburn Rovers. The victory was Athletic's 1,000th win and it was achieved in front of 7,748 fans.

SATURDAY 11TH NOVEMBER 2006

Rockingham Road was the venue for a first round FA Cup tie against non-league Kettering Town. Sean Gregan made his debut for the Latics, scoring the only goal of the first half. The second half was a ding-dong affair until Paul Warne and Neal Trotman put the Latics 3-1 up but the Poppies fought back to 3-3. It looked all set a replay but Chris Hall came on as a late substitute to score an amazing winner.

SATURDAY 12TH NOVEMBER 1898

Pine Villa played their first fixture at the Shiloh ground, which was on a plot of land behind the Rifle Range pub on land now occupied by the Elk Mill.

FRIDAY 12TH NOVEMBER 1982

JW Lees Brewery stepped in to help save the club from financial ruin. In a deal worth £500,000, the brewery bought the Boundary Club and Sports Hall Complex, thus discharging bank overdrafts and other debts. The package included a five-year sponsorship for the ground, programmes and shirt advertising.

SATURDAY 13th NOVEMBER 1920

A 5-2 hammering in a First Division game at home to Tottenham Hotspur was enough to leave the Latics next to the bottom of the league with just nine points from 14 games. A George Wall penalty and a goal from William Halligan were the Oldham scorers.

SATURDAY 13th NOVEMBER 1976

Over 9,000 supporters were present to witness Athletic beat Carlisle United by 4-1 in this Second Division game at Boundary Park. Vic Halom scored a hat-trick and David Shaw added the other goal.

SATURDAY 13th NOVEMBER 1982

Athletic made up ground on fourth-placed Wolverhampton Wanderers in this exciting Second Division fixture at Boundary Park. Rodger Wylde scored a hat-trick and John Ryan got the other goal in a 4-1 victory.

WEDNESDAY 14th NOVEMBER 1923

Tommy Walker was born in Cramlington and he scored 23 goals in 158 league games for Athletic in the mid-1950s. His speed made him the winner of many handicaps in the famous Scottish Powderhall athletics meetings. He was also a Methodist lay preacher who played mostly on the right for the Latics. He won FA Cup winners' medals with Newcastle United in 1951 and 1952.

FRIDAY 14th NOVEMBER 1952

Hugh Moffat died in Macclesfield. He signed for Athletic from Burnley for a £490 fee in 1910 and scored ten goals in 162 league games. He played for the Latics when the club finished their first season in the First Division in seventh spot and accepted an invitation to tour Austria and Hungary. Moffat was capped by England in his time at Boundary Park.

SATURDAY 14th NOVEMBER 1970

The Latics beat Lincoln City 4-2 at Boundary Park with Jim Fryatt scoring a hat-trick. The win cemented Athletic in third place in the Fourth Division and kept the Blues well on track for their promotion charge. New signings for the assault were Maurice Short, Bill Cranston, Don Heath and Barry Hartle.

SUNDAY 14TH NOVEMBER 2004

Athletic visited Ship Lane to take on non-league Thurrock Town in the first round of the FA Cup. The Latics dominated the game which was decided by a Chris Killen penalty in the 48th minute.

WEDNESDAY 15TH NOVEMBER 1967

Wayne Harrison was born in Stockport. After working through the youth team and after only six first team league appearances and one goal, he was snapped up by Liverpool who shelled out £250,000 to make him the most expensive teenager ever. It never seemed to work out at Anfield and Wayne retired through injury in 1991. He tried a stint of management with Accrington Stanley but retired in 1999.

THURSDAY 15TH NOVEMBER 2007

Oldham Council rejected Athletic's bid to redevelop Boundary Park stadium, although they passed plans to upgrade the Broadway Stand. The club were hoping for a positive result after the four years of preparation on the project to take both the football club and the town forward. Doubts over figures in a traffic survey as well as the large scale of the development and the loss of open space and amenities were the reasons given for the rejection.

SATURDAY 16TH NOVEMBER 1895

The first-ever Pine Villa match to be recorded occurred on this day when Villa beat Boothill Albion 'A' by a score of 4-0.

TUESDAY 16TH NOVEMBER 1937

Goalkeeper Jimmy Rollo was born in Helmsdale, Sutherland. His career at Boundary Park was hampered by the fierce competition with John Hardie and Johnny Bollands. He made a total of 59 league appearances. Jimmy was a competent keeper whose strengths were dealing with high shots and crosses. Jimmy lost his right leg in an accident in 1989. When he regained his strength he took to travelling the world but his health was failing and he suffered a minor stroke in the summer of 2004 which resulted in him losing his eyesight.

WEDNESDAY 16TH NOVEMBER 2005

Chasetown's FA Cup fairytale run came to an abrupt end at Boundary Park in this first round replay. It was their tenth cup tie of the season and they brought an amazing 2,500 followers to watch the game. Their league games are usually watched by crowds in their hundreds at the Scholars Ground. Goals by Paul Warne, Chris Porter (2) and Chris Hall put paid to any remaining thoughts of a possible giant-killing act. The Midland Alliance outfit had done themselves proud and went on to finish runners-up in the league behind Rushall Olympic.

MONDAY 17TH NOVEMBER 1902

Frank Hargreaves was born in Ashton-under-Lyne. He was to sign for Oldham Athletic three times between 1923 and 1948 and scored 17 goals in his combined 104 league games. A great dribbler, and very clever with his distribution, Hargreaves was appointed second-team trainer in 1933 and was promoted to first-team trainer in 1936.

TUESDAY 17TH NOVEMBER 1987

Athletic reached the fourth round of the League Cup. Having seen off Carlisle United and Leeds United over four games in the previous rounds, the Blues took on First Division Everton at Goodison Park. Denis Irwin scored for Athletic but they lost 2-1 in a closely-fought match.

SATURDAY 17TH NOVEMBER 1990

A 1-0 loss at Port Vale ended Athletic's remarkable record-breaking start to any season. The Latics had gone 16 league games without defeat but it still left them sitting pretty atop Division Two.

SUNDAY 18TH NOVEMBER 1923

Ace goalscorer Ray Haddington was born in Scarborough. In his 126 games for the Latics, he scored 73 times and was thought to be the best striker of a dead ball ever to represent the Boundary Park outfit. He was famed for his ability to score from long range and almost impossible angles. In the 1950/51 season Haddington was transferred to Manchester City for a fee of £8,000.

SATURDAY 19TH NOVEMBER 1927

Wolverhampton Wanderers were the visitors to Boundary Park for a Second Division game. Neil Harris got a brace and Jack King also scored in a 3-0 win which left Athletic sitting in fifth place in the league table.

SATURDAY 19TH NOVEMBER 1938

A hard-fought 3-3 draw at Darlington left the Latics in third spot in the league table after this Third Division (North) game. Ronald Ferrier (2) and Bert Blackshaw got the goals that earned a point.

SATURDAY 19TH NOVEMBER 2005

Chris Porter scored a bizarre hat-trick in the first 23 minutes of the League One game at Griffin Park. Brentford fought back to earn a share of the points and Lloyd Owusu headed home in the 89th minute to level the scores for the Bees.

SATURDAY 20TH NOVEMBER 1909

Leicester Fosse provided the opposition for a Second Division game that Athletic lost 3-0. The win left the Foxes just one point behind league leaders Glossop North End in the table.

SATURDAY 20TH NOVEMBER 1937

Chester City entertained the Latics in a Third Division (North) fixture where 'Taffy' Jones, Paddy Robbins and Bert Blackshaw got the Oldham goals. The result left Athletic two points behind league leaders Gateshead.

SATURDAY 20TH NOVEMBER 2004

The Latics won a nail-biter to leapfrog Barnsley in a League One game watched by just 5,593 fans at Boundary Park. It was Athletic's fourth win in five outings. Chris Killen got two of the goals in a 3-2 win, one of them coming in the 90th minute, and Scott Vernon got the other goal after he headed home a neat flick from Mark Hughes.

SATURDAY 21ST NOVEMBER 1981

A 0-0 home draw with Crystal Palace was something of a rarity in a successful season to date. The game was the first Second Division game where Athletic had failed to score a goal.

WEDNESDAY 22ND NOVEMBER 1989

First Division leaders and league champions Arsenal came to Oldham for a fourth round League Cup game. Athletic did not let their illustrious visitors get into their stride as they turned in one of the best post-war performances by any Latics side.

Andy Ritchie scored on the stroke of half-time and Nicky Henry put his side two up with a 30-yard volley in the 64th minute. In the 74th minute Ritchie scored a glorious stooping header to kill off any hopes that the Gunners had of getting back into the tie. Niall Quinn pulled back a consolation goal but manager George Graham confessed, "The fact is that Oldham were by far the better team".

TUESDAY 23RD NOVEMBER 1965

Neil Adams was born in Stoke-on-Trent. He originally signed for Oldham on loan, but manager Joe Royle went back to his old club, Everton, to make the deal permanent. He paid £100,000 to secure the player's services and he stayed at Boundary Park for five years.

Adams had two spells – a total of 31 goals in 217 appearances, in all competitions – at Athletic and in his first stint was a member of the Second Division championship-winning team, as well as making a Wembley appearance in the League Cup final against Nottingham Forest. He was transferred to Norwich City for £225,000 but returned on a free transfer in July 1999.

WEDNESDAY 24TH NOVEMBER 1965

Andy Barlow was born. Barlow was a local lad who joined Athletic as an associate schoolboy having previously played for Hulme Grammar School, and he went on to make 302 appearances, scoring 16 goals. He was a member of the team that won the Second Division championship in 1991 and was the player who was hacked down by future boss John Sheridan of Sheffield Wednesday, which gave the Latics the penalty that ensured promotion with probably the last kick of the season.

TUESDAY 24TH NOVEMBER 1981

Athletic travelled to Loftus Road to play on Queens Park Rangers' new artificial pitch. The 0-0 Second Division draw was significant as Oldham were the first visiting team not to concede a goal on the pitch.

SATURDAY 24TH NOVEMBER 1990

The Latics played Bristol Rovers at Bath City's non-league ground, their home ground for the season. They put in a poor performance and lost 2-0. Derek Brazil, on loan from Manchester United, made his league debut for Athletic. The loss surrendered the top spot in the Second Division to West Ham United.

SATURDAY 25TH NOVEMBER 1922

Sheffield United won a First Division game 2-0 at Boundary Park and the result left the Latics with just 11 points and just one place above bottom club Arsenal, who had a worse goal difference.

SATURDAY 25TH NOVEMBER 1972

Notts County lost at home to Athletic by 4-2 in a Third Division match that left the Latics just four points away from league leaders Bolton Wanderers. Colin Garwood got two goals while David Shaw and Ian Robins chipped in with a one apiece.

SATURDAY 25TH NOVEMBER 2006

Over 13,000 were at the Galpharm Stadium to watch Huddersfield Town take on the Latics in League One. The away side were in devastating form and came away with a 3-0 win, their fourth successive league victory. Old boy Luke Beckett was celebrating his 30th birthday but his old team-mates gave him not so much as a sniff at goal. Gary McDonald opened the scoring and Chris Porter side-footed his 11th goal of the season to double the score. Paul Warne got the final goal as hundreds of home fans walked out in disgust, some to protest outside the ground.

TUESDAY 26TH NOVEMBER 1935

Jimmy Thompson was born in Chadderton. He joined the club as a schoolboy when he was 16 years old and then signed as an amateur in 1957. Thompson went on to score 19 goals in his 110 league-game career at Oldham.

TUESDAY 26TH NOVEMBER 1957

Manchester City FA Cup finalist Tony Henry was born in Houghton-le-Spring, Newcastle. Tony signed from Bolton Wanderers in 1983 and was a regular first teamer in his four years with Athletic and was voted Player of the Season by Athletic fans in the 1984/85 campaign. A versatile player, he was Joe Royle's first cash signing for £21,000. He went on to play in 207 games, scoring 27 times before his transfer to Stoke City in December 1987.

SATURDAY 26TH NOVEMBER 1960

A thrilling FA Cup battle emerged at Saltergate with over 9,000 in attendance. The 4-4 draw was achieved with strikes from Peter Phoenix, Bobby Johnstone and Bert Lister (2) to bring Chesterfield back to Boundary Park for a replay.

SATURDAY 26TH NOVEMBER 1977

The Latics were third from the bottom of the Second Division with only 12 points. They made the trip to Field Mill and beat Mansfield Town 2-0. The result spurred on Athletic to a run of 12 league games undefeated. The season saw Mike Bernard come and go, as well as the signing of Steve Taylor and Steve Gardner. Pay rebel Alan Groves was transferred to Blackpool with the promise of First Division football, but they eventually got relegated and he ended up playing in the Third Division!

MONDAY 27TH NOVEMBER 1920

After the previous home game, a 2-2 draw with Burnley, the Latics made the short trip to Turf Moor only to suffer a 7-1 hammering by the hosts. The result put Burnley one point clear at the top the First Division. Around 20,000 people watched the mauling in which the only Oldham goal came from George Wall.

FRIDAY 27TH NOVEMBER 1987

Manchester City defender Earl Barrett was captured for a bargain £30,000 fee. He went on to become an outstanding defender and was sold for a massive profit when he moved to Aston Villa for £1.7m.

WEDNESDAY 27TH NOVEMBER 2002

Burton Albion was the venue for a second round FA Cup replay. After a 2-2 draw at Boundary Park, a sell-out crowd of 3,416 were at Eton Park to hopefully witness a giant-killing act. The 600 or so fans from Oldham had other ideas.

Clyde Wijnhard put the Latics ahead in the 50th minute, only for Burton to equalise six minutes from time to take the game to extra time. The non-leaguers then went ahead in the 110th minute but David Eyres forced the game to penalties and Carlo Corazzin got the winning spot kick to send Athletic through by 5-4.

SATURDAY 28TH NOVEMBER 1925

Athletic recorded their biggest FA Cup victory when Lytham, from the West Lancashire League, visited Boundary Park. There was a minute's silence before the game in remembrance of Queen Alexandra who had died earlier in the week. Played in atrocious conditions, the home side hit three goals in the first ten minutes in this first-round match. The 6-1 half-time lead turned into a 10-1 victory. Lytham's team contained six amateurs and fitness started to tell near the end of the game in front of a 10,093 crowd.

MONDAY 28TH NOVEMBER 1960

Fans' favourite Andy Ritchie was born in Manchester. In his two spells with the club he scored a total of 107 goals in 278 games and was a major contributor in the glory years from 1989 to 1991. In his first season he was voted Player of the Year by both the Supporters' Association and the Junior Latics.

He was given a free transfer to Scarborough in August 1995 but came back as player-coach in February 1997. In May the following year, he succeeded Neil Warnock as Latics manager. New chairman and owner Chris Moore predicted the club would be back in the First Division but it wasn't to be and the popular Ritchie was dismissed. He will remain one of the most popular players ever to grace Boundary Park.

SATURDAY 28TH NOVEMBER 1964

Jimmy McMullen, Oldham Athletic manager from May 1933 until May 1934, died in Sheffield. He was only in charge for one campaign but led his team to ninth place in Division Two, a commendable finish. Two FA Cup ties against Sheffield Wednesday attracted huge gates and netted large receipts – almost £6,000 – for the club. His team lost 4-2 to Bolton Wanderers in the final of the Lancashire Senior Cup, which was played at Maine Road. When he left Oldham, he took up the position as Aston Villa's first ever manager in 1934. He lasted a year at Villa Park – then moved to Notts County – before completing a five-year stint at Sheffield Wednesday.

SATURDAY 28TH NOVEMBER 1990

Athletic entertained Middlesbrough in a home First Division fixture. Mark Brennan made his debut. Without a league win for almost two months, the Latics brushed aside any possible Boro threat with considerable style. Ex-Brighton goalkeeper John Keeley played only his second game for Athletic and could not have expected such an easy afternoon as he was a virtual spectator. Almost 12,500 fans watched Neil Pointon score his first Latics goal while Gunnar Halle, Graeme Sharp and Neil Adams completed the 4-1 rout.

SUNDAY 29TH NOVEMBER 1885

Goalkeeper Howard Mathews was born in Roadend, Worcestershire. Mathews made 368 appearances for the Latics between 1908 and 1926. He played between the sticks for 14 seasons of football for Oldham. At only 5ft 9ins, he made up for his lack of height with his superb agility and positional sense. He was still playing for Halifax Town in his 45th year.

TUESDAY 29TH NOVEMBER 1960

After the previous Saturday's thrilling 4-4 draw at Chesterfield in the FA Cup, the Latics limped miserably out of the competition with a humiliating 3-0 replay reverse in front of over 13,000 expectant fans at Boundary Park.

SATURDAY 30TH NOVEMBER 1907

When Athletic played Leeds City in the Second Division, the half-time score was 1-1 but the Latics were late coming back onto the field. The referee blew his whistle two or three times so he allowed Leeds to kick-off towards the Rochdale Road end. Captain Jimmy Fay saw what was happening and raced down the steps to the field to give chase on the Leeds winger Croot but he couldn't stop him centering for Gemmell to score. Oldham eventually won the game 4-2.

SATURDAY 30TH NOVEMBER 1985

A 2-2 draw at Fulham was achieved with goals from Roger Palmer and Ron Futcher. The point gained was the only one acquired during a winless run of ten games which saw the Latics drop from second place in the Second Division table to fifth from bottom.

OLDHAM ATHLETIC
On This Day

DECEMBER

FRIDAY 1st DECEMBER 1989

Athletic entertained Blackburn Rovers in the Second Division and won 2-0. The game was insignificant as all the feeling on the night was for Joe Royle who had been offered the chance to talk to Manchester City about their vacant manager's job. Some dedicated Oldham fans paid for an advertisement on the official scoreboard that read: "Please Joe – Don't Go". Obviously, Mr Royle took it all to heart and refused to disappoint the anxious supporters as he decided not to leave the Latics midway through the season.

SATURDAY 1st DECEMBER 1990

After two defeats the Latics bounced back to register their record Second Division win for the season when they hammered Brighton & Hove Albion 6-1. Ian Marshall struck two while Tony Henry, Neil Adams, Neil Redfearn and Andy Ritchie completed the rout.

SATURDAY 2nd DECEMBER 1922

Athletic were bottom of the First Division when they made the short trip to Lancashire neighbours Preston North End. The Lilywhites ran riot with a 5-1 scoreline to send most of the 12,000 fans home happy, except for the poor souls who travelled from Oldham. Billy Hibbert got the lone goal for the sorry-looking Latics.

TUESDAY 2nd DECEMBER 1997

Bottom-of-the-league Carlisle United visited Boundary Park and went down 3-1. Paul Rickers, Stuart Barlow and Lee Duxbury got the goals which left Athletic in third spot in the Third Division.

TUESDAY 3rd DECEMBER 2002

Athletic travelled to Selhurst Park for a fourth round League Cup game. Having got there by beating Notts County at home and Derby and West Ham away, expectations were high. The Latics were unbeaten away from home but in a poor performance, they lost 2-0 to Crystal Palace, even though the Eagles had played the second half with ten men after Danny Granville was sent off for violent conduct.

SATURDAY 4TH DECEMBER 1976

Fulham seriously dented Athletic's promotion aspirations with a 5-0 mauling at Craven Cottage in this Second Division match. The disappointing result left the Latics three points off a promotion spot, but they still had a game in hand.

SATURDAY 4TH DECEMBER 2004

The Latics maintained their new ruthless streak with their seventh win from the last eight games. The lambs to the slaughter were Leyton Orient who were on the wrong end of a 4-0 scoreline in this second round FA Cup game. Chris Killen caused most of the upset with a hat-trick but Lee Croft completed the misery for the Londoners as he walked round the Orient keeper to stroke the ball into the empty net. Athletic earned a money-spinning third round home tie against Premiership side Manchester City.

SATURDAY 5TH DECEMBER 1981

A 3-1 win over Grimsby Town resulted in Athletic attaining their highest league placing for 30 years. Goals from Paul Heaton, Jim Steel and a penalty from Rodger Wylde were enough to move them up into second place in the Second Division.

SATURDAY 5TH DECEMBER 1987

Athletic went to Dean Court to take on AFC Bournemouth for the game in which Frankie Bunn made his Latics debut. Bunn was a saint, and a sinner, as he won a penalty, but also conceded one to give the Cherries a draw. The spot kick from Nick Henry and a goal from Tommy Wright earned Oldham a 2-2 draw, leaving them in 20th place in the Second Division.

SATURDAY 6TH DECEMBER 1941

It was World War II and the third season of wartime football. On the day when the half-time announcement was that the Japanese had attacked Pearl Harbor, the Latics played Halifax Town and won 6-2. Only 479 people turned up to watch the game, the second lowest-ever attendance for a first team game at Boundary Park.

SATURDAY 6th DECEMBER 2003

Bogey team Blackpool pulled off their second win of the season at Boundary Park, in the FA Cup. John Eyre and Jermain Johnston got the Latics goals but it wasn't enough as the Seasiders hit five to complete a convincing 5-2 away victory.

WEDNESDAY 7th DECEMBER 1898

Stalwart Teddy Ivill was born in Little Hulton and joined Athletic after a trial in 1924. He struggled to get into the team in his earlier years but established himself in the 1927/28 season, clocking up an amazing 224 consecutive matches in a five-year spell.

He totalled 285 Latics appearances and scored three goals, the last against Huddersfield Town in the FA Cup in 1932. The gate of 30,607 was triple the usual attendance. The Terriers equalised two minutes from time and went on to win the replay 6-0. Ivill was granted a testimonial in the same year then left to join Wolverhampton Wanderers for a fee of £1,700.

SATURDAY 8th DECEMBER 1979

Simon Stainrod got the only goal of the game to beat Chelsea in a Second Division game watched by a 10,000-plus crowd. The result was a serious dent to Chelsea's promotion push.

TUESDAY 9th DECEMBER 1970

Athletic were knocked out of the FA Cup by non-league opposition for the first time. After a 0-0 draw at Simonside Hall in the second round three days earlier, they went down 2-1 at home to South Shields. It was a disgraceful performance and Maurice Whittle was so disappointed that he took off his shirt and threw it to the ground in disgust when he was substituted.

SATURDAY 10th DECEMBER 1938

A 4-2 win over Wrexham was achieved with goals from Ernest Wright, Ronald Ferrier (2) and David Halford. The result left Athletic in third spot in the Third Division (North).

TUESDAY 11TH DECEMBER 1990

It was a night to forget as the Latics went to Sheffield United for a Full Members' Cup tie and went down, big time, in a 7-2 reverse. Roger Palmer and Ian Marshall got the insignificant goals in front of 3,144 fans.

TUESDAY 11TH DECEMBER 2007

Plans to develop Boundary Park were finally approved by Oldham Council. The £80m plans included 693 new homes, a fitness centre and a landmark hotel. Fans turned out in numbers on the night to support the vote after previously organising a peaceful protest march to the ground.

SATURDAY 12TH DECEMBER 1925

Stockton was the venue for an FA Cup second round game in which Athletic triumphed 6-4. Bert Watson scored four, while an Albert Pynegar strike and Sam Wynne penalty completed the rout. Having beaten Lytham 10-1 in the first round, the Latics had now hit 16 goals in two cup games.

SATURDAY 13TH DECEMBER 1947

Athletic lost 1-0 at home to Mansfield Town in an FA Cup game watched by 21,067 disappointed supporters. The Latics fans had witnessed a 6-0 hammering of non-league Lancaster City in the previous round and were definitely expecting better from their team.

TUESDAY 13TH DECEMBER 1949

Crewe Alexandra were the visitors to Oldham for an FA Cup replay which ended in a 0-0 stalemate. It needed a second replay before Athletic eventually won through 3-0. The pitch and weather on that day meant that the Latics went through 24 pairs of shorts and 26 jerseys to complete the match.

SATURDAY 14TH DECEMBER 1907

A 4-1 win over Gainsborough Trinity left Athletic sitting proud on top of the Second Division. A hat-trick from Frank Newton was complemented by a single goal from Joe Shadbolt.

SATURDAY 14TH DECEMBER 1991

Everton were the visitors to Boundary Park for a First Division game which ended in a 2-2 draw.

SATURDAY 15TH DECEMBER 1990

Athletic bounced back from the humiliating Full Members' Cup hammering at Sheffield United to record a handsome 4-1 home Second Division win over Wolverhampton Wanderers. It was the Latics' first league double of the season. Earl Barrett, Andy Ritchie and two goals from Roger Palmer did the damage.

TUESDAY 16TH DECEMBER 1969

Bert Gray died in Blackpool. The 6ft 3ins goalkeeper became Athletic's most capped player with nine Welsh international appearances, helping his country to Home International success letting in just a solitary goal in the three matches. He notched a century of league games for the Latics before moving on to Manchester City in 1927.

MONDAY 17TH DECEMBER 1934

England World Cup winner Ray Wilson was born in Shirebrook, Derbyshire. One of England's best post-war full-backs, Wilson spent a year at Boundary Park making 25 league appearances. Having been appointed club captain, he suffered an injury and the skipper's role was handed over to Maurice Whittle. Wilson was given a free transfer to Bradford City but was to retire soon after as his injuries took hold.

SATURDAY 18TH DECEMBER 1948

A second round FA Cup replay was staged at Boundary Park against Walthamstow Avenue. After a 2-2 draw in the initial game in London, Athletic ran out 3-1 winners with goals from Eric Gemmell and two from Ray Haddington. Over 26,000 supporters watched the contest.

SATURDAY 18TH DECEMBER 1993

Athletic forced a hard-earned 1-1 draw at Coventry City in a Premiership fixture. Paul Bernard scored the equalising goal for the Latics in a game watched by almost 12,000 fans.

SATURDAY 19TH DECEMBER 1908

A Second Division home game against Leeds City was watched by a crowd of around 8,000. It was a very one-sided affair as the Latics ran out 6-0 winners; Frank Newton got a hat-trick, Finlay Speedie scored a brace and 'Snowy' Hamilton converted a penalty.

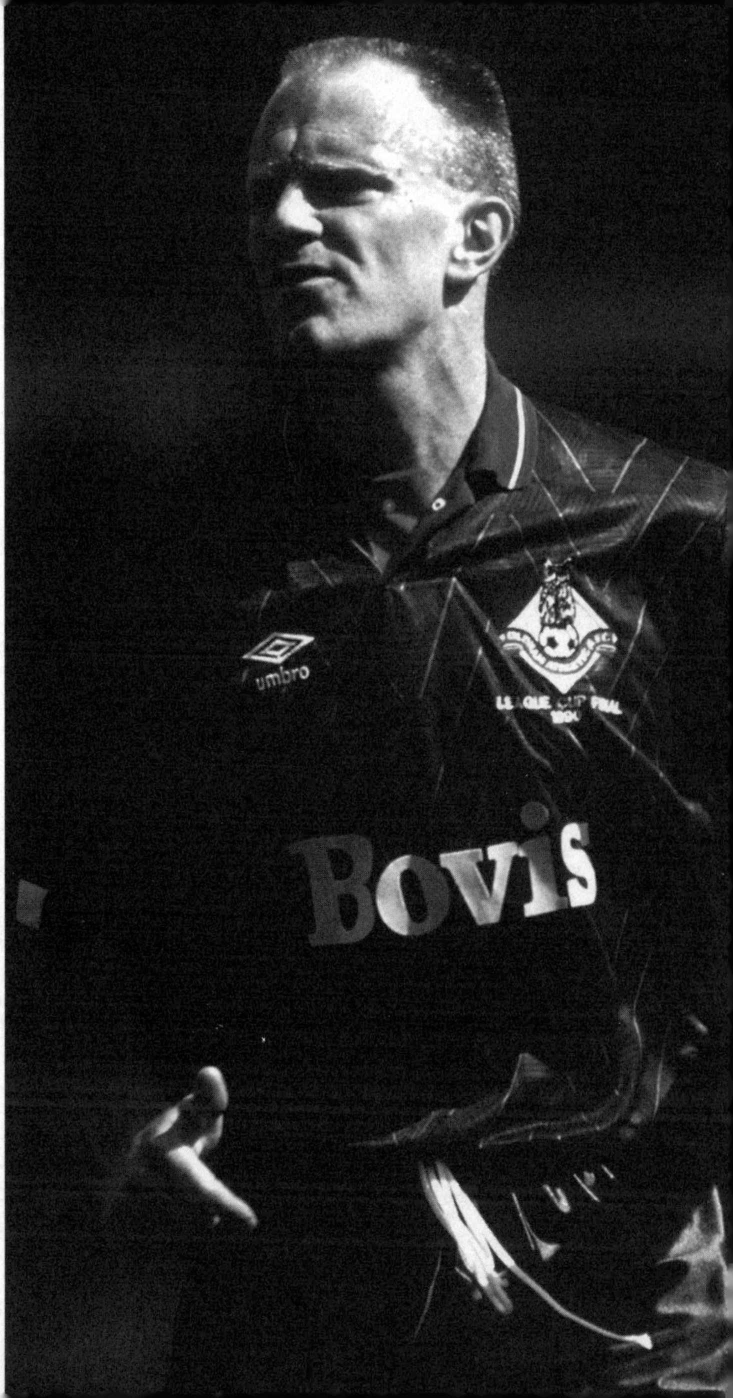

ANDY RITCHIE WAS ON TARGET AGAINST WOLVES IN DECEMBER 1990

FRIDAY 19TH DECEMBER 2003

Oldham Athletic Administrators PKF convened meetings of the club's shareholders and creditors for the purpose of proposing a Company Voluntary Arrangement (CVA). If the creditors and shareholders approved a CVA for the club on 8th January 2004, it was anticipated that the Football League would approve a transfer of the Football League membership to the proposed purchasers of the club at its next board meeting on 15th January 2004. To completely devastate the Latics, manager Iain Dowie also walked out on this day to join Crystal Palace.

MONDAY 20TH DECEMBER 1897

Left-back Reg Freeman, who made the step up from amateur football to the First Division, was born in Birkenhead. He played 104 games for Athletic and his debut against Bolton Wanderers at home on 15th January 1921 resulted in a 0-0 draw which was the start of a six-match unbeaten run.

SATURDAY 20TH DECEMBER 2003

In a match where David Eyres and John Sheridan took over the Latics reins after Iain Dowie had walked out, the Latics pulled off a shock Division Two victory over Queens Park Rangers; Oldham's first win in over two months. It left Rangers boss Ian Holloway fuming. Ernie Cooksey and John Eyre got the markers against QPR's goalkeeper, and future Oldham player, Chris Day.

TUESDAY 21ST DECEMBER 1965

At a board meeting, chairman Harry Massey stepped down to vice-chairman and Ken Bates was appointed his successor. Mr Bates was to bring many changes to the set up at Boundary Park and his intentions were made clear immediately his Silver Cloud Rolls Royce arrived at the ground. He wanted success in a field that he admitted he knew little about and stated: "Europe is our goal, and it can be done". He was to introduce the *Boundary Bulletin*, a brash new programme never before seen in the league. He certainly put his money where his mouth was by completing the signings of Frank Large, Reg Blore, Dennis Stevens, Ian Towers and Bill Asprey.

FRIDAY 21st DECEMBER 1990

A comfortable 5-3 success over Plymouth Argyle took Athletic back to the top of the Second Division table. With 11,296 supporters at Boundary Park egging them on, Roger Palmer and Neil Redfearn got two goals apiece and Earl Barrett chipped in with the other.

SATURDAY 21st DECEMBER 2002

Athletic became the first team to score at Chesterfield since August. When Fitz Hall scored the match-winning goal in a 1-0 victory, he ended the Spireites' Division Two home run which had seen them go 742 minutes without conceding a goal at Saltergate. The win was the Latics' first in nine games and ended their mini crisis.

WEDNESDAY 22nd DECEMBER 1937

George Kinnell was born in Cowdenbeath. Although he was only at Boundary Park for three months, Kinnell quickly became a fans' favourite with his eight goals in just 12 league games. Athletic made a quick profit on his sale to Sunderland but the move did not go down well with the Latics faithful who had hoped that he would stay.

WEDNESDAY 22nd DECEMBER 1948

One of the few foreign players around at the time when he appeared for Athletic, Ryszard Kowenicki was born in Poland. He played in 42 league games for the Latics between 1979 and 1981 and scored five goals, mostly spectacular long-range efforts. His peculiar claim to fame was his unusual long throw-in technique which resulted in him following through and landing face down on the field. Unbelievably, his toes always remained behind the line, thus making the throw legal. The execution provided the Oldham fans with endless laughs!

SATURDAY 23rd DECEMBER 2006

Over 10,000 people, the biggest home gate of the season, were in full voice at Boundary Park as they watched Athletic take on Northampton Town in a League One game. The Latics were in a play-off spot and needed points to consolidate their position. The Cobblers fell to their heaviest away defeat of the season with a 3-0 loss. The important goals came from Gary McDonald, Chris Porter and Andy Liddell.

SATURDAY 24TH DECEMBER 1910

David Wilson was captain of the Athletic team that took on Sheffield Wednesday at Boundary Park. When he took the toss for ends before the game, he faced his brother Andrew who was captain of the visiting team. It was a rare occurrence for two brothers to captain First Division teams. The Latics won 1-0 and Wilson later went on to become manager of Oldham in the 1927/28 season.

WEDNESDAY 24TH DECEMBER 1962

Southport were the visitors to a cold and snow-covered Boundary Park and were humbled 11-0 – Athletic's record score to this day which equalled their highest-ever number of goals in one game. Bert Lister led the goal feast with six, Colin Whittaker scored a hat-trick, while John Colquhoun and Bob Ledger completed the rout. Athletic had led by 9 goals as early as the 53rd minute in this remarkable Fourth Division game. Master schemer Bobby Johnstone was the architect of proceedings and was very unfortunate not to get on the scoresheet himself in front of the delirious 14,662 fans.

SATURDAY 25TH DECEMBER 1920

A bottom-of-the-First Division battle ensued at Boundary Park. With Yorkshire rivals Bradford Park Avenue propping up the league it was crucial for the Latics to win. William Halligan got the only goal of the game as Oldham moved fourth from bottom after this 1-0 victory.

WEDNESDAY 25TH DECEMBER 1929

Bradford Park Avenue were hammered 5-1 at Athletic in a game watched by an 18,000-plus gate. Stewart Littlewood and Lawrie Cumming got two apiece and utility player Matt Gray got the other goal to keep Athletic in second place in the Second Division.

THURSDAY 26TH DECEMBER 1935

Athletic sustained their heaviest defeat ever in a Third Division (North) league game. Tranmere Rovers scored 13 goals with the visitors hitting four in reply. On the previous day, Athletic had beaten the Rovers at Boundary Park by a 4-1 scoreline.

SATURDAY 26TH DECEMBER 1981

A 3-0 reverse at home to local rivals Blackburn Rovers ended Athletic's Second Division unbeaten home record. The defeat started a poor run where they scored only 12 goals in 19 games across all competitions – a run which included five consecutive games without scoring.

WEDNESDAY 26TH DECEMBER 1990

The big Second Division Boxing Day clash at Upton Park pitched first-placed Athletic against second-placed West Ham United. With the majority of the 24,950 partisan crowd cheering on the Londoners, the Hammers ran out worthy winners on the day by 2-0. The result meant a switch in league positions for the two sides.

SATURDAY 27TH DECEMBER 1980

Grimsby Town were the visitors to Boundary Park in the first match ever to be played with the new under-soil heating in use. The Mariners won 2-1 with Rodger Wylde hitting the lone goal for Athletic. The result left the home side in 20th place in the Second Division on 19 points while Grimsby sat nine positions – and 6 points – higher.

SATURDAY 28TH DECEMBER 1974

Table-topping Manchester United had only lost three of their 24 Second Division games when they brought their star-studded team, with six internationals, to Boundary Park. While their illustrious visitors were 'lording it', the Latics were struggling at the wrong end of the table. Both teams were new to this level of football, Athletic just gaining promotion whilst United had been relegated from the top flight.

The Latics took the lead in the 11th minute when Ronnie Blair headed in George McVitie's centre but referee T. D. Spencer waved play on as he thought the ball had hit the angle of the crossbar, rather than the stanchion, before it bounced back out. Justice on the day was done though, as Maurice Whittle scored the only goal of the game from a penalty in the 68th minute. A 26,356 crowd watched the match, the result of which inspired the Latics to crawl away from the relegation zone.

TUESDAY 28TH DECEMBER 2004

This League One game went true to form as goals from Scott Vernon and Neil Kilkenny were enough to dispose of visiting Peterborough United. The win extended Athletic's unbeaten home run, which went back to October.

TUESDAY 29TH DECEMBER 1969

Manager Jack Rowley was given the sack for the second time at Oldham. He had brought in England World Cup winner Ray Wilson as captain and David Shaw, Maurice Whittle, Mike Faulkner, John Bingham and Jim Beardall, but his new signings failed to inspire the team and he paid the price, as Athletic were in 22nd place in the Fourth Division. Bradford Park Avenue propped up the league with a meagre 13 points from 24 outings while Workington were one place, and one point, below the Latics on 14 points from the same number of fixtures.

SUNDAY 29TH DECEMBER 2002

Athletic ended Crewe's ten-match unbeaten run with a fine 2-1 victory at Gresty Road in front of 9,006 supporters. The win hoisted the Latics above the Railwaymen into fourth place in Division Two and maintained their undefeated away league record. A goal from Carlo Corazzin and a David Eyres penalty were enough to seal the win.

SUNDAY 30TH DECEMBER 1923

Tommy Bell was born in Heyside. He made his Athletic debut as a 23-year-old in a second round FA Cup tie at home to Doncaster Rovers on 14th December 1946 – a 2-1 defeat for the Latics. When Billy Wootton replaced Frank Womack as manager Bell fell out of favour, but some good performances and a switch of position from left- to right-back got him back into the first-team. Bell was also an ever-present during the 1950/51 season when George Hardwick took over as player-manager. He made 181 appearances for the Latics before moving to Stockport County. His son, Graham, later played for Athletic. Tommy died in Chadderton on 21st November 1988.

WEDNESDAY 30TH DECEMBER 1970

Coach Jimmy Frizzell was appointed the new manager of Oldham Athletic, replacing Jack Rowley who had been fired the previous day. Rowley had been working on a 4-4-2 formation to bolster the defensive attributes of the team. Walter Joyce was put in charge of the reserves. Under Frizzell's guidance the team started to improve and he pulled a master stroke in February when he bought Jim Fryatt from Blackburn Rovers for £8,000. His goal poaching helped pull Athletic out of the danger zone and also gained Frizzell a new two-year contract.

THURSDAY 31ST DECEMBER 1936

Peter Phoenix was born in Manchester and began his career at Oldham playing as a left-winger. He was equally at home as a wing-half and was a popular figure with a great shot. He spent four years at Boundary Park scoring 31 goals in 178 games, before moving to Rochdale in exchange for Colin Whittaker.